DIRTY JEWESS

dirty JEWESS

A WOMAN'S COURAGEOUS JOURNEY
TO RELIGIOUS AND POLITICAL FREEDOM

by

SILVIA FISHBAUM

with

ANDREA CODDINGTON

URIM PUBLICATIONS
Jerusalem • New York

Dirty Jewess
A Woman's Courageous Journey to Religious
and Political Freedom
by Silvia Fishbaum
with Andrea Coddington

Copyright © 2018 Silvia Fishbaum and Andrea Coddington

Translation: Gabriel Levicky, Stacy LaRosa, and Silvia Fishbaum
Edited: Rebecca Spence and Dr. Rochelle G. Saidel

Typeset by Ariel Walden

Printed in Israel

First Edition

ISBN 978-965-524-277-5

Urim Publications
P.O. Box 52287
Jerusalem 9152102
Israel
www.UrimPublications.com

Library of Congress Cataloging-in-Publication Data

Names: Fishbaum, Silvia, author. | Coddington, Andrea, 1975- author.
Title: Dirty Jewess : a woman's courageous journey to religious and political freedom /
by Silvia Fishbaum with Andrea Coddington.
Description: First edition. | Brooklyn, NY : Urim Publications, [2018]
Identifiers: LCCN 2017056880 | ISBN 9789655242775 (hardcover : alk. paper)
Subjects: LCSH: Fishbaum, Silvia. | Jewish women—Czech Republic—Biography. |
Czech Americans—Biography.
Classification: LCC DS135.C97 F46 2018 | DDC 305.892/404373092 [B] —dc23 LC
record available at https://lccn.loc.gov/ 2017056880

"The Girl with her Doll."
Original charcoal drawing, 1933, by Lajos Feld.
(*Photo credit: David Feldman*)

Contents

	Acknowledgments	9
CHAPTER 1	The Only Jews in Our Village	13
2	From Porubka to Kosice	18
3	Beginning Anew In Kosice	25
4	Jewish Blood	30
5	Discovering My Old Teacher	37
6	The Only Choice	42
7	Dreaming of Love and Escape	51
8	Attempting to Escape	58
9	Playing it Safe	66
10	Saving Money for My Escape	72
11	A Second Chance to Escape	80
12	Touchdown	92
13	Moving to New York City	100
14	Meeting Mr. Right	107
15	Getting Married	116
16	Living My Dream	122
17	Traveling to Israel and Italy	132
18	Homecoming	136
19	Why Is This Happening?	145
20	After the Fall of the Iron Curtain	155
21	The Saddest Chapter of My Life	164
22	Moving On	168
23	Festival of Light	181
	Epilogue	189

Acknowledgments

It was Andrea Coddington who first brought my story titled ZIDOVKA (Dirty Jewess) to life. It was published in Slovakia in 2010 by Ikar and quickly became a platinum bestseller, selling more than 25 thousand copies in its first year with long waiting lists in every single library around the country.

I have enormous gratitude for her encouragement and support in nurturing this book from its inception. Andrea has never been exposed to Judaism before and she took to it like fish to water. Together we threaded those deep, dark corridors down memory lane. We laughed and cried along this great adventure.

This book would not have been possible without the desire to keep the memory of my parents, both Holocaust survivors, alive.

I also wish to honor the memory of my childhood art teacher, Ludovit Feld, for he became the inspiration to fulfil my late husband's wish.

My intention was to have the book in English to let my children, family and friends know what it was like growing up in the post Holocaust communist Czechoslovakia, for those who stayed behind the iron curtain – the plight of the second generation. I would like to assure everyone that, yes, your dreams do come true and one should never give up.

Never did I envision such a success of my memoir, as I hoped to stay somehow anonymous. Therefore most of the names in the book are changed, although all the locations are authentic.

I would like to thank Gabriel Levicky for his enthusiasm in helping me create the first English draft.

Likewise I am genuinely indebted to Stacy La Rosa for her invaluable passion to find my voice in English.

Acknowledgments

A big hearty thanks go to Rebecca Spence for her efforts and suggestions in shaping the first copy of the manuscript.

A boisterous and thunderous thanks goes to Dr. Rochelle G. Saidel. Her brilliant wisdom, comments, and savvy feedback helped bring the book to its final version.

I would like to express my deepest gratitude to my entire family, relatives, friends and peers who surrounded and supported me. I am truly lucky to be encircled by all of you.

Last, but not least I would like to acknowledge my gratefulness to Pearl Friedman, editor at Urim Publications, for her input and beautiful, encouraging words.

*In memory of our loved ones
and all those who live in our hearts for eternity.*

I, Sophia Manisevicova, would like to thank you
for holding this book in your hands.
And the next time we meet, on the very last page,
I want you to know that my real name
is Silvia Fishbaum, and this is the story of my life.

☙

The Only Jews in Our Village

Porubka, Czechoslovakia Fall, 1961

MY PARENTS HAD EAGERLY expected a son who would perpetuate our family's name and traditions, and it was equally important to them to have a son who would recite the *Kaddish* memorial prayer after they were gone. According to *Halacha*, or Jewish law, only males are required to perform this ritual.

However, my parents had three daughters: the oldest is the beautiful Melanie, the middle one is Hanka, and I am Sophia, who was known as the little rabble-rouser.

I am darker-complexioned and a bit more impulsive than my two sisters. Because of my temper and coloring, people joked that I must have fallen out of a Gypsy wagon on its way down the dirt road in our rural village of Porubka. My parents, Simone and Yaakov, must have found me and done a good deed, a *mitzvah*, by taking me in as their own. Since I was their last girl, my parents would have the barber cut my hair so that at least I would resemble a boy.

I had no clue what it meant to be Jewish.

One Friday, when I was six years old, my mother seemed somewhat different. She was a bit more at ease than her usual nervous self. It was no wonder, as her soul had been filled with pain and sorrow for so long, and her sense of serenity had been snatched away from her many years before. But on that particular day, she appeared less tense, and even smiled a little. Although she was a beautiful woman, you could see traces of horror and suffering in her eyes. She could never really laugh, and she seemed hesitant to fully embrace life. Constantly on guard, in silent tension, she went through her days with strength, dignity and poise.

"Shabbos is a delicate gift from God," Mother loved to say, as if giving us a peek behind the veil of mystery of Shabbat, or Shabbos. "We honor Shabbos and Shabbos honors us back."

She knew quite well that we were absorbing every word, listening as though we could never get enough. But while we were enraptured by her tales, we also knew how much was left unsaid.

I always cherished Fridays. From the wee hours of the morning, my mother would be even busier than usual in the kitchen, so that come evening, my family could sit together around the Shabbat table, relaxing, watching and enjoying the sunset. My father would play board games, cards, and dominoes with my two sisters and me, or read us story books and tell tales about our small country of Israel. While Mother was busy at the stove, she would nod approvingly at the whole scene, receiving pleasure or "schepping nachas," as she would say. The kitchen was her kingdom, always clean and tidy, with spice racks neatly placed beside fresh loaves of homemade bread, which she enhanced with her own handmade embroidered covers. The aroma penetrated every nook and cranny of our peasant house.

"Honoring Shabbos has always kept Judaism alive," my father would say. "We hold on to it, we lean on it no matter where in the world we are, whether drowning in our sorrows, or filled with gratitude. And we, as a people, are there for others as well."

Father was not a talkative man. He never went to great lengths to explain his motives to his family, but we knew very well that we meant everything to him. And still, he made sure to devote time to friends and neighbors, too. He was always ready to help, offer advice, or lend money to someone in need.

On this particular Friday, he seemed especially joyful.

"This day we sanctify God!" he exclaimed. "Shabbos, holiday of holidays!" "But why is Shabbos such a special day?" asked eight year old Hanka.

"Because God created the world in six days and on the seventh day he rested. That is what Shabbos is all about. It is a day of rest, of not working," Father explained.

"Is it because we have to gain new strength so we can work the next six days of the week?" Hanka asked. We had frequently heard our father's classic Story of Creation.

"Exactly," Mother replied proudly.

"Even if I am not tired?" asked my oldest sister, Melanie.

"The most important thing in life is balance. In order to work well, you must also rest," Father said. He himself happened to be a workaholic, and a perfectionist as well. It was important to him that whatever he did must be just so. He had a natural talent for precision, down to the most minute of details, and he expected the same from others. In addition to being a master roofer, he owned a huge vineyard just behind the village, which, other than us, was the most important part of his life.

"Mely, you are your father's daughter. It is undeniable," Mother said, taking one baking sheet from the oven, and sliding in the next one. She was obviously referring to my sister's personality that was similar to our father's. "If, for example, a pillow is not placed exactly as it should be, you automatically start fixing it," she said.

"Yes, you are right," said Mely, eight years my senior. "I too am a perfectionist. Perhaps one day I will do nothing but rest," she said, with a smile.

I could tell that something was bothering her. She didn't know where to begin. After taking a deep breath, she repeatedly turned towards our parents, then back to my sister and me. I felt as if I were watching a ping pong game. At the same time, she kept straightening chair covers, stretching starched table cloths, and bending down to pick up invisible specks of dust from the floor. She was always delicate, like a well-loved doll. Finally, she mustered up the courage to speak. "Father," she said quietly. "May I ask you a question?"

"What is it, my dear?"

"Why is it that we are the only family in Porubka that observes Sabbath on Saturdays? Why don't we go to church on Sundays like everyone else?"

"Because we are Jews and they are not," he replied. As Mely formulated her next question, his kind face grew stern.

She stepped forward and raised the pitch of her voice. "But why *us*? Why only us?"

Even at my young age, I stood there frozen, feeling chills run through my entire body, almost not wanting to hear the answer.

"To be a Jew is a privilege," Father answered. Then the conversation really started to heat up.

"Oh really, is that what you think it means, being treated like scabby dogs?" Melanie blurted.

Her body was shaking all over. "Is that considered a privilege?"

No one would ever have expected such a negative remark from such a sweet girl. "Melanie!" Mother shouted.

"What?"

"Stop it immediately." Mother's smile disappeared. She was clearly shaken by my sister's outburst and rebellious attitude.

"They hate us. The whole village hates us! Nobody likes us. Why only us? What have we ever done to them?" Mely broke down in tears.

"It is not that bad," Mother said. "It will change with time, or you will get used to it. And we are not the only Jewish family, even though you think so. Many have perished and are gone forever, but a lot of us are still here." Although we girls had no clue what Mother meant by this, we knew it was not good.

"We are the same, yet different in our beliefs," Father answered, much calmer than before. "Those who go to church on Sunday have their laws and rules to follow, and we have ours."

Father was a good man. All he wanted was for everyone to be happy, and his greatest desire was for peace on Earth. I remember how upset he would become when the neighbors quarreled over the fence and about their hens apparently rummaging in each other's gardens. Simple, silly spats were not important to Father, and he would not engage in such frivolity. He was a man of substance and compassion, and could always see the bigger picture. When he saw his daughters suffering, he also suffered. Mely's feelings and outrage pained him, but he felt helpless. There was nothing he could do to comfort her or protect her from the outside world.

We were the only Jewish family in this Christian village of Porubka, and he knew that to others, we would always be "those Jews."

Father was about to say *Kiddush*, the ceremonial blessing over the wine that welcomes in Shabbat. He always prayed in Hebrew. At that time, I believed that Hebrew was not a language for everyday conversation, but just a language of prayer. Now I know differently.

"If only those others could see how happy we are for who we are, and how *we the Jews* celebrate Shabbos with such joy and devotion," Father said. "Then they might understand us a little better and not hate us so much." He wanted to end this unpleasant debate as soon as possible, and stop arguing with his own daughter.

But Mely was relentless. "They hate us!" she screamed.

"That's enough." Mother stepped in to rescue Father. "The time will come when you will understand it all."

This was typical of our mother. Just like her. With one of her classic sentences, such as, "You are not mature enough, but one day it will all make sense," she had put an end to all the questions, accusations, and explanations. And, as always, she was right.

The matches in her hand were a clear indication that Mother was about to light the Shabbat candles. It was also an unspoken signal there would be no further questions or answers, neither from her, nor from Father. We all knew that there was to be no more discussion.

CHAPTER TWO

ᐟᒡ

From Porubka to Kosice

O UR LITTLE VILLAGE OF PORUBKA, in the Eastern part of Slovakia, was slowly recovering from the devastation of World War II. But despite a few barren years, I remember our childhood as relatively carefree. I remember small peasant homes with flower gardens in the front and back yards; farms with vegetable patches, and grain and potato fields, separated by alleys of various fruit trees, where everyone was equal – everyone, except us. We had the same farming land with the same chickens, geese, ducks, cows, and goats, and also the same water well and the same outhouse as everyone else. However, the simple fact that my father didn't raise pigs, and that he was named Yaakov, rather than John, George, or Michael, made us outcasts. We were Yaakov's daughters – the daughters of that rich, stinking Jew.

My father was rich, which made us doubly cursed. He owned a huge vineyard on many acres of land. On the side of the house he had built a sizable workshop, where he employed many young village boys as apprentices in his trade. He was famous throughout the region for his quality wine, and this vineyard determined our future back then. A year consisted of cutting back the vineyard in freezing February, planting young grapes during the spring, endless journeys up and down the hill, pruning fresh buds, and tying them until June. By the end of summer, we would all celebrate the joy of the harvest.

Our entire home and yard smelled of grapes. We produced Beaujolais wine, fresh grape juice, and other wines that were fermented in barrels and then poured into bottles for sale. Yaakov's wine had an outstanding reputation, not just for the quality of his product but also for how well he treated his customers. People flocked to him from all around the region just to get a taste of his wine. It practically sold itself and he worked mainly through word of mouth. Father was passionate about his wine and made every batch with love, care, and consistency. But because of the success of his vineyard, we lost the chance to go to America or Israel like the other Jewish families in our region. As with any blessing we receive, there is often a downside. For my family, losing the chance to emigrate was the price we paid for what the vineyard provided.

I was born under the Star of David, so there was no need to have it sewn onto a coat or affixed on my forehead. Everybody already knew that I was Jewish. How I hated it when the kids on the street, thinking I wasn't looking, would whisper things behind my back. The more courageous ones would wag their fingers, indicating that I was a *persona non grata*, stick out their tongues and yell, "stinking Jew." In those moments, all I wanted to do was disappear. I was so hurt and embarrassed by their taunts that I wished the earth would just swallow me up and take me away from this torment and cruelty.

At those times, I would run to the shelter of my home, where I could hide from the outside world. I would curl up in our cozy living room, furnished with chairs, a couch, and a small coffee table decorated with a vase of dried flowers. A lovely picture of the Tatra Mountains hung on the stenciled, painted walls. My home was real and gave me great comfort. It was my sacred space. By contrast, Israel, that dreamed-of land we'd heard so much about, seemed to be so out of reach, so untouchable: a storybook world filled with miracles.

Here in Porubka, I couldn't understand why the other villagers behaved so differently towards me, especially the other children. Was it my imagination? Or were they constantly poking fun at me and calling me names? Whether I wanted to be one, or whether I chose to be born as such, how did they know I was a Jew? And what did the non-Jews see that made me stand out? Were there horns on my head? Was my blood a different color? I felt just like everyone else, but even at the age of six, I realized that others did not see my family and me the way that I saw us. Why was it they preferred for us to be known as a *Jewish* family, rather than a winemaker's family, or a roofer's family, which is what we were? There were no real answers, neither at home nor outside.

We were not your typical family in a small village that had only one street with an upper and lower end. We were the only ones with a motorcycle, which my father owned before the war. We were also the only ones who did not cross ourselves in front of the crucifix when we passed the church in the center of the village. However, there was one time when this was not completely true.

Our Melanie, oh, how she wanted to blend in, to assimilate and conform. She wanted to be just like everybody else, the ones she called "The Normals." One day, on the way home from school with her classmates, she inconspicuously crossed herself in front of the crucifix. The old matrons dressed all in black, who spent their days gossiping on the bench, began to laugh, and the rest of Melanie's entourage felt uncomfortable. Those old women made faces at my sister. They couldn't figure out how to react to what they had just witnessed. Neither could Melanie. She didn't mean any harm, but her intentions were misunderstood. Rumors traveled fast in our village, and sure enough, word got back to my mother before poor Melanie could make it home. She hadn't even walked in the front door when Mother confronted her.

"You can't do that!" Mother said. "What do you mean?" Melanie asked.

Despite being beautiful, Mely wasn't a good actress. Her face was laden with emotions, and she was unable to hide her shame, which was mixed with pride. Forbidden fruit tastes the best, even if it is slightly rotten, unripe, full of worms, or stolen from a nearby neighbor's tree.

"You know quite well what I am referring to," Mother continued in the same breath. "But I . . ."

"No buts."

"Mother, all the boys and girls and everybody in the village cross themselves," she continued. "Let them! But not you! Not us!"

Melanie took a deep breath. "Please don't start again with your litanies of one day understanding it all, figuring it out, or that someday this will make total sense."

"We are not everybody! Don't you ever do that again, do you understand? Never!" Mother's voice and hands trembled as she spoke.

"But Mother, why? Why don't we go to church on Sunday? Why can't we recite *The Lord's Prayer*? Why not us?" she pleaded.

"Because we are Jews. I do not want to repeat this endlessly. They have their cross, which they believe is theirs to carry all their lives. Do not try to take it away from them, Mely. Let them have it, let them cross themselves as many times as they wish. Just don't you ever do it again."

Mother's voice was firm and no one dared to oppose her. Finally Mely entered the house and closed the door behind her. As she passed by,

Mother took her hand and continued. "We have our burden and we are a minority, so we have to defend ourselves. We must never, ever give up. You are a beautiful girl and you should be proud of yourself, your heritage, and everything that we are and stand for," Mother said passionately.

"That's exactly what I would like," Melanie conceded.

"There is absolutely nothing to be ashamed of," Mother wisely said.

Melanie started sobbing, as if she had betrayed her own people. She sobbed out of guilt, anger, shame, and pain. She took my mother's words seriously, scared that she had hurt her. Ever since then, whenever we approached the crucifix, Mely would lower her head and turn her gaze in the other direction. She said she would rather drop dead than hurt our parents again. They left her alone with her bowed head, knowing that one day, she would walk proudly through the village, flaunting the golden Star of David that she now hid on a thin chain under her clothing. They knew that one day she would look straight into people's eyes, holding her head high.

After that scene with my sister, I became so scared of the crucifix, it was as if it were the devil himself. Whenever I passed by, I would turn my head in the other direction, too petrified to even catch a glimpse.

My mother had tried in vain many times to convince my father that we should follow other Jewish families to seek a better life. There was not much to expect in post-war Communist Czechoslovakia. My mother begged so repeatedly that it felt like thousands of times to me. "Let's go," she would say, recalling the *Shoah*. She believed we deserved better. "Enough is enough," she would say. "Look at the nationalization and normalization steps we have to take. It will do us all in." The Communists were equally as horrible as the Nazis, maybe even worse.

My mother was desperate to leave. It was a constant presence around her, both in her waking hours and her dreams. Quite possibly, she was trying to escape from herself or her past. I know that feeling, as I am just like her. When something bothers me, I jump on a plane. When faced with a situation I'm unsure about, my first impulse is always to flee. Nothing helps, not even well-meant advice from close, trusted friends. I run away, as though I can somehow escape my own shadow or reflection in the mirror, always hoping that this time I will finally leave all my worries behind, or at least shake them off for the moment. But without fail, they are always there, waiting for me upon my return. This is my usual pattern, finding out that there are situations that only time can heal, and that I have to learn patience.

Despite Father's firm objections, Mother took us to Prague to apply for a visa to the United States. Mother's cousin Margaret, who lived in Brooklyn, New York, used to send us parcels filled with beautiful dresses and blue jeans. One such package included the affidavit, the official invitation needed in order for us to emigrate. We were so close to leaving. We had the money, and all we had to do was pack and embark on our new life in the United States. But no matter how hard Mother tried to sway him, Father would not budge. His beloved vineyard in Porubka had won. So we remained in our farmhouse where Mother cried and cried for days. Trying to appease her, Father promised that everything would work out for the best. He had been unwilling to give up his vineyard, but he would soon be forced to do so.

The harvest season had just begun, and as a true wine-making family, we eagerly awaited its arrival. That year turned out to be one of the richest harvests ever with the grapes juicier and heavier than all of the previous years. It looked like better times had finally arrived. Everything was ready. Workers flocked to Yaakov to make some extra money, and he had plenty of jobs for everyone. His favorite quote was, "Working with wine is like being on a merry-go-round. You move in circles all the time." He was so busy and excited, it was wonderful to watch him.

It was early autumn 1961, and I remember it clearly because it was the same year that I started first grade. As excited as Father was about the grape harvest, I was just as excited to begin elementary school. But all of that excitement turned into heavy darkness in a split second, as if by the wave of a magic wand. The Communists came and put an end to Father's merry-go-round. They confiscated and then nationalized his vineyards. It was as bad as, if not worse than, if they had chopped off his legs. From that moment on, Father remained bitter. He never forgave himself for not listening to our mother, and for not allowing her to fulfill her American dream. Now it was his turn to cry.

"My dear Simone," he said to my mother. "*Oy vey, what tzures*, what misery has fallen upon us!"

"Now you see where your stubbornness got us," she said. "You should have listened to me and paid attention to my warnings. What is going to happen to us now?" she cried.

"Don't worry," Father said. "I will take care of the family. We still have a roof over our heads, and I have my trade. It will all work out, I promise."

"*Bubbe meise*, it's a fairy tale!" Mother cut him short in Yiddish, sighing. "I am terribly sorry," Father said.

"Leave me alone," Mother said, and pushed him away. "Nothing good can come out of this. We have lost our vineyard and this is only the beginning. I don't trust the Communists."

"Do you think it doesn't bother me too?"

"Crying over spilled milk won't help us," Mother continued.

Father attempted to calm her down, but she adamantly refused. Now it was her turn to be stubborn. After she went to bed, he remained in the kitchen, staring ahead in a stupor, sipping on his wine, searching for truth. Perhaps Father believed that *in vino es veritas*. Our parents mainly communicated with each other in Yiddish when they didn't want the children to understand. We did manage to pick up bits and pieces here and there, and even with our meager understanding of Yiddish, we got the message that something horrible had happened, or was about to.

I am not sure whether my father ever managed to discover the truth in wine, but my mother put her foot down and we began packing. Yaakov Manisevic packed his furniture, his daughters, his wife, and all of his hopes and dreams. My first grade teacher, Comrade Tulekova, never had the chance to get to know me because by January, we were already leaving Porubka.

There was one more thing. We were well off, but our father did not trust the country's financial system, including the banks. He wouldn't take anyone's advice when it came to depositing money there, and he preferred instead to always hide stacks of bills under his mattress. Apparently, it was a sizable amount. But after the Communists devalued our existing currency, they introduced their new money, and all the wealth that Father had accumulated throughout his life lost its value. Yesterday's, money became worthless.

As for Mother, it was not wealth that she craved. She simply wished to live among her own people. Without our vineyard, without money, and without a synagogue to worship in, she felt lost in Porubka. Our connection to our home had been completely severed and we all felt disconnected, with Mother feeling it the most. Family clans of Naftulovitzes, Mendelovitzes, Hershkovitzes, Chaimovitzes, Jacobovitzes, Zelmanovitses, Schwartzes, Schermans, Kleinmans, Feldmans, Ackermans, Rothmans, Vizners, and Weinbergers had all left forever, gone just like our vineyard.

Someone had taken over the little shul in Porubka and converted it to a family house.

Whoever had returned from the horrors of the Holocaust in 1945 had tried to bury their memories of the past. They'd done their best to lock them away, hopefully forever, so they could gather their strength for the next leg of their journey. All of the survivors had already left Porubka. Now, finally, it was our turn.

There was, however, one other Jew who remained in the area. His name was Avrumele Gubner, and he was an old bachelor from the nearby village of Koromla. Avrumele was a loner who never married, as there were no Jewish girls left. But through all of his suffering, Avrumele never lost his faith. It was of utmost importance to him that the woman he chose as his wife would be Jewish. While the center of Porubka was marked by a crucifix, in Koromla, the most recognizable landmark was undoubtedly Avrumele. He was simply known as *The Jew*, like a signpost that people referred to when describing where they lived. "Oh, I live two houses down from *The Jew*," people would say, or "I live diagonally across from *The Jew*." When I went to visit him many years later, it was still the same, as if nothing had changed. Avrumele stayed in Koromla for the rest of his life.

❧

CHAPTER THREE

Beginning Anew In Kosice

S HABBAT HAD BEEN a big event in Porubka, but my mother managed to make it into an even grander feast in Kosice. We never lacked for anything in the pantry or on the table. The refrigerator was always full, and the balcony held whatever didn't fit in it. Three times a week, Mother went to the local farmer's market to buy whatever fruits and vegetables were in season. However, for exotic fruits such as tangerines, bananas, pineapples and grapefruits, we all had to stand in line at the local fruit market, waiting for our allotment of one kilo per person. Most importantly, nothing could be wasted. If we so much as threw out an overripe tomato, Mother would say, "If only I could have had this to eat in the camp . . .," referring to the concentration camp she claimed to have survived by sheer miracle. With that kind of guilt, we made sure to never again make the mistake of wasting food.

Like many concentration camp survivors, my mother had a lifelong obsession about food.

Every time the refrigerator started to look a bit empty, she would immediately shop, carry the heavy load of groceries home and then cook for hours. She suffered from recurring nightmares that reminded her of the fear of hunger and thirst that she had known during the Holocaust.

Every Friday night, she would turn our home into a culinary kingdom. She baked and cooked from early in the morning, but I must admit that I didn't much care for her traditional, homemade roulades and babkas. I considered them old-fashioned and far inferior to the napoleons, creamy cones, punch cakes and seven-layer-cakes that I bought at the local pastry shop. Today, however, I would give anything for a taste of my mother's roulades and babkas filled with cocoa, poppy seeds, and walnuts. I wouldn't trade them for the most decadent desserts in the world.

On Fridays everyone could smell her traditional, braided challah bread from one end of Czechoslovakian Army Street to the other. She was so proud as she checked the progress of her dough rising up to the edges of the pan. That is how I will always remember her, standing in front of the oven, holding a pan with a big golden baked challah, the aroma penetrating every pore of my body. She also used to buy live chickens, ducks and geese that she would bring to the *shochet* on Zvonarska Street for slaughter. At home she would continue a salting ritual that was required to make them fully kosher. The Shabbat table was always beautifully arranged with lovely place settings, fresh bouquets of flowers in the summer, and dried flowers in the winter. The small apartment was always clean and tidy, and everything was properly prepared according to tradition.

On Friday evenings, my sisters and I would wear our most beautiful dresses. Just before sunset, Mother would place the candles in her silver candelabra, lovingly light them, and with her head covered by a lace kerchief, she would welcome the Sabbath with her prayers. This is a ritual that has been carried on by Jewish women for centuries, and I still remember Mother explaining that through the flame of a burning candle, we become directly connected to God. Through this connection, all of our prayers and wishes are fulfilled.

I can still smell the *cholent*, the traditional Shabbat stew of beans, beef, vegetables and barley, steaming on the table. We couldn't wait to dig in, but first Father would recite the Kiddush. Then he would drink some wine, before passing the cup around so we could all have a sip. After Kiddush, he would say the blessing over the challah, which was placed on a silver platter under an embroidered cover from Israel. Upon finishing the blessing of the bread, he would take the first piece for himself, then slice a piece of challah for each of us. Only after that were we allowed to eat our Shabbat meal. This is a ritual I have always loved and always will.

I first fell in love with Shabbat when I was a little girl. At seven years old, I would pray hard that the day would never end, and when Saturday night arrived, I would look forward to the next Friday. Friday had always been my special day and it was also a very special day for my entire family. Even now, as an adult, I still feel the same way. At first, I didn't understand why Fridays were so special. I was this little restless girl and all I knew was that my whole family would gather together around the dinner table, no matter what. Whether we were feeling sick or well, whether there was sorrow or happiness, we stuck to this ritual. Fridays were so powerful that they seemed to hold a spell over us. They were superior, untouchable by strangers, and deaf to the sounds of the outside world.

Fridays were simply ours without fail.

In Kosice, I couldn't get used to the noises of the city, such as the rumbling of Tram #6 right in front of our apartment building. I also couldn't get used to the clock bell, tolling each hour, or the commotion of Marathon Square, which stood in stark contrast to the old, small, peaceful park near our old home.

Kosice had been one of the most prominent and populous Jewish communities in Czechoslovakia before World War II. However, by the time we arrived, the former *kehilla*, or community, of 14,000 had been reduced to 500 people who had either survived or managed to remain during the war. The city's synagogue was open for prayer, and a small restaurant that still prepared kosher meals remained in business, employing a traditional kosher butcher. This meant everything to my mother, in the same way that my father's vineyard had meant everything to him.

I attended a new elementary school on nearby Hviezdoslavova Street. It was there that I met my new classmates as well as my new teacher, Comrade Tulejova. Even at the tender age of seven, I believed that since my previous teacher's name had also begun with the letters T-u-l-e, I had to abandon all hope of ever becoming a teacher myself. In Porubka it was Tulekova, and in Kosice it was Tulejova. With my name, Manisevicova, I stood no chance.

My classmates at the new school didn't understand why we Jews burned candles in our kitchen every Friday night, and they would ask annoying questions. In response, I'd make up lies because I didn't know how else to answer. I was not a good liar; I told them that we had no electricity in our kitchen, knowing that everyone else around us did. The truth was that I couldn't come up with a better explanation.

The simple fact that I was Jewish seemed to give my classmates free rein to point their fingers at me, stick out their tongues, curse, and even spit on me. At times it seemed worse than in Porubka. I often returned home from school sobbing, unable to withstand all the shouting or hair pulling, while my classmates searched for my "horns." Every time I heard the words "stinking Jewess," I wished with all my heart that they could see and feel how much it hurt. I wanted them to know how painful and absurd their claims against me really were.

To this day, I believe that they themselves didn't know why they were against the Jews. What compelled them to act in this manner, and why? Was it something that came with their mother's milk, or did they just want to fit in, to feel superior to someone else? What was that "something" that made strangers hate me so, and exhibit such cruelty?

Today, things really haven't changed as much as we'd like to believe, and Jews are sometimes still scapegoats in some parts of the world. So what was it that motivated them? Envy? Hatred? Human nature? Is there something inside all of us that guides our behavior? What makes some act out in negative ways, while others do not? Is this a characteristic we all possess, and if this is so, why can some control and overcome it, while others cannot? There are as many answers as there are people on this earth, and for every answer, a whole new crop of questions appears.

"Equal, yet different." I remember my father saying those exact words after I lost my first, best friend, Ildiko. Ildiko was a beautiful, blue-eyed blonde girl who lived with her parents and older brother in our courtyard. They moved to the city shortly before us from a nearby Hungarian village. Ildiko and I were inseparable. We were almost like twins, always holding hands, going everywhere together. When the courtyard froze during the winter, we skated there for hours on end. We were oblivious to the cold because we had each other. We would do spins, jumps, countless circles, figure eights, and twists, wearing shiny skates on high-laced, white boots. But one day, Ildiko's mother approached her daughter and whispered something in her ear. That was it. From that moment on, my Ildiko would never give me her hand again. No explanation was necessary. It was as clear as the ice I was skating on.

Luckily, I had one courageous defender at school, a boy by the name of Arpi Ziga. Arpi was a handsome Gypsy boy, and I thought he was the coolest kid in Kosice. (We later learned that Gypsy is considered a pejorative and the correct term is Sinti or Roma.) He may have even had a little crush on me, but if he did, he could never tell me – after all, I was Jewish.

One morning, as I entered the classroom, I noticed out of the corner of my eye something written in white, covering the entire blackboard. "Sophia is a Dirty Jewess," it said. I stood there, motionless and paralyzed, and then I burst into tears. At that moment, without any prompting, Arpi got up and quickly erased the hateful message. Then, without any explanation, I sat down next to him and shared the same desk. We had a mutual understanding that was so genuine, and I immediately felt relaxed. How grateful I was that someone had finally stood up for me, when for so long, I had had no voice. I didn't know then that so-called Gypsies also were discriminated against by the local population.

As it is with children, yesterday's tragedies and dramas were forgotten by the next morning. There were some moments, however, when I felt angry at the whole world. This feeling would swell from within, and at those times, my mother would try to comfort me and calm me down. "One day it is going to be fine," she would say. "You will get used to it." She stressed that if I thought someone was causing me pain and hurting me, I knew nothing about real pain. "The day will come when you will understand the difference between hurtful words and hurtful actions," she would say. I wished the day would come when she would tell me everything, and I would finally understand what she had been referring to during all of those years.

꙳

CHAPTER FOUR

Jewish Blood

Czechoslovakia, Poland, Germany, Spring, 1944

I AM A CHILD of Holocaust survivors. We Jews carry the legacy of the Holocaust, forever etched into the very fiber of our beings, with memories smeared in blood. Is this really part of being the chosen ones? I often wonder. Or is it, as some of our rabbis preach, God's concept of love, a test for God's most beloved? I might never understand it, perhaps one day I can forgive the Holocaust, but I will never forget. How is it possible that the world allowed this to happen? Did everyone turn a blind eye, or a deaf ear, to what was occurring all around them? What kind of a man could commit these atrocities against his fellow man? And what kind of a person could stand silently by, watching? Was everyone oblivious?

For me, the Shoah is not just another chapter in a history textbook. It is not just the sickening nausea that pervades my body, or the shaking of my head in disbelief when I hear the stories or see the pictures. It is my genes. It is my heritage. It is my mother.

It was the spring of 1944, during the second deportation wave of Eastern Slovakian Jews, when German soldiers took Mother's family to a concentration camp. At some time in early April, right after Passover, the Hungarian soldiers, allies of Germany, raided Porubka and deported all of its Jewish families to a brick factory in Uzgorod, Ukraine. Aware of the grave danger, my grandparents attempted to hide my mother at a beauty salon in Uzgorod where she had been apprenticing to become a hairdresser. As it turned out, this provided only an illusory sense of safety.

Mother wanted so much for her family to remain together that she couldn't bear hiding out. And so she voluntarily surrendered. She was taken to the brick factory, where she joined her mother and father, her ten-year-old brother Mayer, her sixteen-year-old sister Blanca, and her oldest sister Sara, who was twenty at the time. Thus, Mother's entire family, all the Jakubovitzes, were reunited.

I learned this story watching a VHS tape of my mother's testimony for the Survivors of the Shoah Visual History Foundation. She recorded it in 1993, when Steven Spielberg, who had recently won the Oscar for Schindler's List, established the Shoah Foundation to collect survivor testimony from all over the world. Since that time, the Shoah Foundation, now housed at the University of Southern California, has collected visual testimonies from 52,000 Holocaust survivors living in 64 countries worldwide.

It took me seventeen years to finally gather the courage to watch my own mother's testimony. Wrapped in a warm blanket, sipping green tea, I inserted the videotape and pressed play. Seeing my mother's face appear on the screen, I felt as jumpy as the old VHS player I had dragged out of the closet. As she spoke her first words, goose bumps ran up and down my spine. There she was, with her short, dyed brown hair, wearing a black and yellow sweater, and on her ring finger, she wore the same gold wedding band that I still wear to this day.

"We spent six weeks at the brick factory," she said, beginning to open up. "Apart from the ever present fear of our uncertain future, life continued on, slowly, with a false appearance of normalcy. We couldn't do anything other than wait, knowing nothing and fearing everything."

It was obvious just how difficult it was for her to talk about her experiences. She hesitated and paused between sentences. She was forever at a loss to find the right words to describe what was in her heart. Her horrific past had completely destroyed any sense of peace within her soul. After several weeks at the brick factory, my mother and her family were transported to Auschwitz.

"They crammed us into those cars like animals, without any room to move," she recounted. "We had to urinate and defecate right where we stood, and no food or water was provided. We traveled like this for three days and three nights until we reached Auschwitz. They ordered us to get out at Birkenau, where the selection started. They shaved us completely, distributed our striped uniforms, wooden shoes and this is how . . ."

Mother's voice trailed off there.

At the selection ramp, the human cargo was divided according to sex. Those who had survived the trip were ordered to undress. Strong-looking individuals were selected to work and violently separated from their families. But the majority of those on the train ended up in the gas chambers, herded in by SS men with huge, barking dogs, ready to tear apart anyone who tried to resist.

Mother could hardly talk about her father, my grandfather, who was among those instantly sent to the gas chamber. The selection process had been conducted under the supervision of the infamous Dr. Josef Mengele, known as the "Angel of Death." With an almost unnoticeable bend of his finger, snug in his black leather glove, Mengele would point left or right, deciding who would live or die. His decisions were final.

"Sara, Blanca, my mother and I were trying to stick together as much as we could," Mother continued, her voice subdued. Her throat rasped, and her eyes glazed over in that strange way I recognized from my childhood. She paused to gather her strength, then took a deep breath. "Our mother was together with us, my sisters and me, and since she was still young and looked healthy, she was not taken away from us . . . yet," Mother said.

But her brother, who was crying inconsolably, had been separated from the family.

"Poor Mayer stood alone," she said. "Mengele took his hand and offered to help him find his mother. Together they went checking row by row, until they came to us. Mayer grabbed my mother's hand, and we understood then that their fate was sealed. At first, we were unaware of exactly what had happened to them, but a few days later it dawned on us: we had become orphans. That animal. . . ." Mother whispered, as she recalled what had happened.

Listening to her words, I remembered how frightened she would become when she noticed a man in uniform. Suddenly it all made sense. For a long time after the war, she would have panic attacks whenever she saw a policeman, a military officer, or any public figure of authority. Even the mailman's postal uniform scared her. Before a dropped spoon hit the floor she would cringe. As a child, I worried that at any given moment I might scare her so badly that she would have a heart attack.

"Twenty-year-old Sara soon followed those sentenced to die," Mother continued. "She was not good for any type of labor, and she was deemed imperfect. She limped a bit, and was selected for immediate extermination. Only Blanca and I remained."

I imagined my mother, standing there in her coat affixed with a yellow Star of David, waiting and praying, watching the transport train depart.

"We ended up in the women's barracks in the A-camp, and our duties were to select clothing. We separated whatever was good from what needed some mending and what was not useful anymore. That job actually saved my life. There was a *Kapo*, a Czech-born female guard named Smidova, who had picked my sister and me out of the crowd, much to our surprise. Perhaps she liked the way we looked?" she asked.

"In the clothes barracks, nicknamed 'Kanada' (largely because even though it was a completely hellish existence, it was relatively bearable), we managed to steal small items of clothing. We would then smuggle them out, and were able to trade with the Polish inmates working in the kitchen for an extra piece of bread or a potato." When talking about her hijinks, she smirked a little. Once, though, she almost got killed doing it.

"There was this SS woman, Brandl, who used to perform unannounced spot checks on us every week. The whole camp was terrified of her. Once I had stolen a pair of hose and stuffed them into my coat to make them look like shoulder pads. Brandl caught me, and all hell broke loose. She started kicking me, beating me. You cannot even imagine. The beating continued until I lost consciousness. As if this weren't bad enough, I was transferred to the shoe selection area, which was even worse, since now I had to work outside," she testified.

I could tell that Mother was carefully selecting her memories and choosing her words. She was unwilling to reveal the intensity of the abominations she had witnessed and endured. While watching and listening to her story, I wondered how much more remained unsaid.

"We were exposed to beastly, inhumane conditions, unbearably long early morning and late night lineups, regardless of the weather, where anyone still in possession of their sanity wished they were dead. By the time they finished counting the prisoners, sometimes taking three to four hours, *oy vey*, it seemed like an eternity. If not for the extra pieces of bread from those Polish women, I would not be here today. Even the youngest and strongest women in the camp at times would faint, dropping down like flies. Some of them never got up again," she remembered.

For the longest time, I had been unable to grasp why food was such an important part of Mother's life. Now it all made sense. Haunted by these memories and living in constant fear of starvation, it was no wonder she couldn't enjoy life. In fact, it was a miracle that she was able to adjust to so-called "normalcy" at all. Survivor's Syndrome had marked her life, as well as mine, forever.

Growing up, I wanted desperately to know what had happened to my grandparents, as well as the other members of my family I'd never met. But I was never able to unravel the mystery. Mother's survivor's guilt had seeped through her every word and deed, and she never spoke of the ones we lost, or of the horrors she had suffered. Believing it was in her best interest, I never asked questions. It was enough that she was there for me and my sisters, holding on strong, with her battery of pills and doctor's appointments.

"It must have been a miracle that we survived, especially the death march, when we walked through the snow and ice in freezing temperatures to Ravensbrück, and from there, [transported] farther to Neustadt-Glewe [a sub camp]. They wouldn't even let us eat the snow. During the night we slept in a circle, holding our bodies close to each other for warmth. Unfortunately, some of the older women at the edge of the circle froze to death. The younger ones inside the circle somehow survived with that little extra bit of warmth from the other bodies."

"I will never forget how one time my feet froze and got stuck to my wooden clogs, so that I couldn't walk any farther. Some women tried to warm me up by blowing their breath and massaging my feet to separate them from the clogs, but the pain was excruciating. While we were marching, you could see the many lifeless bodies of those frozen to death or shot, since they were unable to continue their journey."

Due to the severe frostbite my mother suffered on that march, she was left with desensitized thumbs, damaged nerves, gastrointestinal disorders, and rheumatism. And yet, she rarely complained. I couldn't fathom how she had survived all of that, and still had gone on to live a full life, giving birth to three daughters. To the Germans, she was merely one of the millions of nameless, faceless, bodies, some identified only by the numbers tattooed on their forearms. But to me, she was my hero.

"For about three months, I worked in Germany at an airplane factory [in Neustadt-Glewe], operating heavy duty riveting machines," she continued. "No food, only imitation coffee that was awful and undrinkable despite our intense hunger. They gathered some grass together with earth and cooked it into a so-called soup. It was impossible to eat. It got caught between your teeth and was very crunchy. Then one day, we woke up realizing we were liberated. First the Americans arrived, then later on the Russians."

By the time my mother was liberated, she weighed less than eighty pounds and could barely walk. But she was alive. The only thing she had the strength left to do was hold her sister's cold, bony hand.

"I remember begging my sister not to touch the bread they were giving us, even though we were so hungry and thirsty, despite dreaming about it every night in the camp," my mother recalled. "We were warned that the food provided might not be safe. Those who did not heed the warnings became quite ill, swelling up in the abdominal area due to an outbreak of typhus. Nearly half of the former camp inmates died shortly after they were liberated, simply because they overate and could not resist the temptation after starving for so long."

Lice-infested and emaciated, my mother and Blanca embarked on their journey homeward.

When they finally reached Porubka, they found a barren space where their family home had once stood. All that remained of their previous life was a few prized possessions they had managed to store at a teacher's house; the rest was simply gone. Standing there, they realized they were orphans, with no place to go and no tears left to shed.

"The house was completely razed," my mother recounted. "The villagers did a good job looting to make sure nothing of value was left behind. They were searching for gold. We were lice-infested, had no strength left, and were so dirty and hungry that people were afraid of us, suspecting we might be carrying diseases. Fortunately, one brave neighbor offered us food and basic health care," she recalled.

But the real miracle for her was reconnecting with my father.

Not many Jews had managed to survive and make it back to Porubka, but of those who did, a few were surprised to find their homes still intact. My father was one of them. He had successfully escaped from a forced labor camp in Hungary, and later joined the Partisan movement. Back in Porubka, he resumed his work as a master roofer. Given the destruction the war had wrought, his services were now in high demand. There were no problems with payments, and his clients often bribed him with freshly baked bread and still warm cow's milk; whatever they could afford.

One afternoon, he came upon my mother, who, as a little girl, used to polish his famous motorcycle. Because he had known my mother and her sister before the war, he took them in and gave them shelter, and during this time Yaakov and Simone fell in love. It didn't matter that he was fifteen years her senior. From that moment on, he never left her side. And while their love might not have been what fairy tales are made of, it was a solid, long-lasting bond.

My mother was not the only one to find her soul mate. Not long after she and Blanca began living under my father's roof, a young Jewish bachelor named Julius Schwartz showed up in Porubka looking for a bride who turned out to be Blanca. They fell in love, got married, and moved to Decin in the Czech region, where Julius found gainful employment. Ten years later, in search of a better life and future, they moved their young family to Chicago.

But first, my own parents got married, lived happily ever after until . . . the VHS tape ended. Wrapped in my blanket, lying motionless on the sofa, I wished I could tell my mother: "Finally, I understand you."

※

CHAPTER FIVE

Discovering My Old Teacher

AROUND THE SAME TIME that I watched my mother's testimony, I thought of my childhood art teacher in Kosice, Ludovit Feld, who had also survived Auschwitz. An early inspiration in my life, Feld had been a talented painter who mentored many aspiring artists in post-war Czechoslovakia.

Though he was a dwarf, we all called him "Our Little Giant, our dear Uncle Lajos." Once I realized that he had lived through the same nightmare as my mother, everything began to make more sense.

I still remember Ludovit Feld's radiant face and loving smile. He looked as if he were constantly trying to cover up his sad history with a sunny expression. If only that were possible. Imagine injecting Botox into your senses, as if to remove the memories of pain, the wrinkles of desensitized nerves. Perhaps that tender smile was only an illusion, a mask of happiness covering the face of such a wise and gentle sage. I will never forget how, pencil in hand, he would instruct us to measure objects before we even attempted to paint them. But, oh, how impatient I was back then. I wanted to paint and draw, not measure. And so I stopped attending his art classes. What a pity.

Many years later, when I returned to Kosice for a visit, I went looking for Ludovit Feld's paintings. I searched and searched throughout the city's museums but found nothing. As brilliant a painter as Feld had been, he was now all but forgotten. That was 1987. In the years that followed, I began researching Ludovit Feld's history, and even interviewed him to learn the details of his life story. He was born in 1904 to a poor, Jewish family in Kosice, one of nine children. A childhood illness had stunted his growth, leaving him a dwarf. Paradoxically, this handicap saved his life.

While imprisoned at Auschwitz, and precisely because he was a dwarf and a talented artist, Feld was appointed by Josef Mengele to be his personal artist. The Nazi doctor was notorious for his obsession with anomalies and deformities. Dwarfs, giants, hunchbacks, the mentally retarded, hermaphrodites, obese men, and well-rounded women fascinated him. In fact, anyone who displayed a genetic disorder caught Mengele's fancy, although his main obsession was with twins. The Nazis mercilessly exterminated healthy people, while those with any dysfunction or deformity became a source of entertainment and amusement. Only in the presence of those with so-called "imperfections" could these brutes feel superior.

Like my mother, Ludovit Feld could have evaded capture by the Nazis. The names of his illiterate parents and eight siblings had all appeared on the deportation list, while his name was missing. For this he could thank one of his former students, a City Hall typist who had been ordered to draw up the list of Jews living in Kosice. Hoping to spare his life, she omitted dear Uncle Lajos. But like my mother, he could not abandon his family. After spending one night alone in his empty apartment, he packed his painting supplies and marched straight to the brick factory.

Mother could have hidden at her hair salon, and Feld could have remained free. Two cities, two brick factories, two fates. But both of them risked everything to be with their families.

At the brick factory, Feld joined nearly 13,000 other Jews, who were jammed together in filthy, overcrowded conditions. He began to draw the horrifying scenes he saw before his very eyes. While he tried to give the impression that they were being treated like human beings, the high walls, brutal conditions, and armed guards spoke for themselves. The Kosice brick factory was a filthy, disgusting ghetto filled with hopelessness and despair.

Ironically, as a free man before the war, Feld had renounced his religion and converted to Christianity. Much to his chagrin, his own family members had ostracized him, and he felt he belonged nowhere. To the Jews, he was a traitor, and to the Christians, he was a stinking, little Jew. But when he finally found his relatives at the brick factory, they all rejoiced at the sight of him. Feeling bad about how they had spurned him, the Feld family burst into tears and embraced their little giant.

That day, May 15, 1944, was the last time Feld would see all fifteen of his family members. Because his name had been omitted from the deportation list, the Nazis forbade him to leave on the first transport with his relatives. Instead, he left on the third transport, and was stuffed into a cattle car with eighty other prisoners. After three horrific days and nights, the train stopped at Birkenau. When the SS guard asked Uncle Lajos his profession, he responded, "*Ich bin maler*," or, "I am a painter."

On the ramp of life and death, the majority of those who had survived the transport were sent to the left, meaning to the gas chamber, where they would die an instant death. But Feld was sent to the right, meaning that like my mother and Blanca, he had been sentenced to life. After he arrived at Auschwitz-Birkenau, where he became prisoner number A-7740, Feld was not only the subject of Mengele's twisted, depraved experiments, but he was also ordered to draw the experiments performed on other prisoners. Feld, together with Czech illustrator Dina Gottleib and Polish photographer Wilhelm Brosse, documented the horrors and atrocities committed against his fellow human beings.

One can only imagine the bizarre and painful procedures performed on the helpless prisoners of Auschwitz-Birkenau, where Feld, still unable to come to terms with Judaism, called himself a "non-practicing Christian."

In June, 1967, Feld testified about his internment at the concentration camp.

"We had a number of injections given to almost all of our organs, medications were administered, and we were subjected to having our blood drawn countless times," he said. "Almost every day, there were experiments performed on us. Mengele personally supervised the experiments, and he was present almost every day."

"Even though our living conditions were much better than the rest of the prisoners, we experienced great mental anguish, as we knew that we would be killed sooner or later, and our skeletons placed in a biological museum," he continued. "Mengele ordered his SS men to guard me. They supplied me with chalk, pencils and papers. He confiscated all my drawings, and occasionally he dropped by, making sure I was not slacking off," he said. "Because of my height, they put me into the children's barracks, with Mengele's twins. Strangely enough, I had become a father figure to them, even though I did not have any children of my own. Now, I had plenty of them. Once, I confessed my conversion to a fourteen-year-old boy named Kalman Bar-On," Feld remembered. After endless discussions between Feld and Bar-On, they discovered that they were related by marriage. This is the miracle of Jewish geography; when one Jew meets another, they always seem to find common roots.

Bar-On had been deported from northern Yugoslavia. At the ramp, he was separated from his entire family, including his twin sister. Inside the children's barracks, Bar-On befriended Peter Grunfeld, nicknamed Pepiczek, who at age four, was the youngest child on the block. Both of them liked to hang around Feld, whom they clung to, even sharing a bunk. "He became my adviser," Bar-On testified for the Shoah Foundation. "He was well educated, with a sense of humor, but he wasn't a positive person. I would hand over Feld's food to him by reaching, because his own arms were too short."

Despite the fact that Feld was exposed to the same tortuous experiments as the other Jewish prisoners, his fellow dwarfs shunned him. To them, he was a traitor for converting to Christianity. "As I say, everything was upside down," Feld testified. "My own people kept silent, avoiding me, and that murderer Mengele was very nice to me outwardly. Once, after a long and tortuous exam by various specialists, Mengele offered me a cigarette and asked how I was doing," Another time, Feld was nearly killed when he and Bar-On were caught throwing stolen bread over the fence to Bar-On's mother and sister. The SS guards threw dear Uncle Lajos against the wall to be executed. "I can still hear the sound of that bullet passing near my ear," Feld testified. "Luckily for me, someone shouted, 'He belongs to Mengele!' and my life was spared."

The last days at Auschwitz were filled with chaos and anarchy. "We heard explosions and the roaring of falling buildings," Bar-On remembered. "This previously busy and overpopulated camp was suddenly, suspiciously silent. No SS around, but there was no escape possible, since the electric fences were still operating. From time to time, some German soldiers would appear, storm the barracks, order everyone out, and then shoot them."

"One morning at lineup," Bar-On continued, "we were told that we would be released, but we knew it was a trap. Feld and I went into hiding, as he had no chance to survive the anticipated march. With his short legs and decimated body, it seemed impossible. That was, of course, if there were any plans for marching at all again."

Feld had convinced Bar-On and fourteen other boys to stay put, because he was uncertain they were being told the truth, and he feared for their safety. "We were hiding under the lowest, wooden planks of the barracks, closest to the frozen ground for ten days and ten nights," Bar-On went on. "Motionless, hungry, afraid, and in the dark, we listened to what could be heard but not seen. We were the heroes. Feld was our leader, and we had opposed the SS. We were terrified, yet also exhilarated. Our amazing Feld was not only our leader, but our savior," he recalled.

On January 27, 1945, the Russian Red Army liberated the remaining 5,800 prisoners from Auschwitz. According to the Jewish calendar, it was Shabbat Shira, the chapter in the Torah when the entire congregation sings the liturgical "Song of the Sea." This song describes Moses and the children of Israel praising God for the miracle of parting the Red Sea and it holds great meaning for the Jewish nation.

After the liberation, Bar-On wandered alone for several months, before locating his twin sister. Sadly, his parents had perished. In 1947, Bar-On and his sister moved to Israel, where I met him many years later. As for Uncle Lajos, he returned to Czechoslovakia in very poor health. He stayed with his only surviving sister in Bratislava until 1949, and later returned to Kosice, where he settled down and once again embraced his Jewish faith. Concluding his testimony, Feld proclaimed: "Our God saved us . . . I hope my boys are all right. I am not in touch with them, unfortunately, but all I know is that we survived, and we did it together."

✺

CHAPTER SIX

The Only Choice

Kosice, The 1960s

"STOP PUSHING YOURSELF into Heaven like a Jew!" a snotty, old man yelled, as he tried to block my entrance to the tram. I'd heard this insult a thousand times before, but it never lost its sting.

"How dare you?" I spat back. "You don't even know me!"

"What?" the man said, as he lifted his walking stick. In his black work boots and smelly blue overalls, covered with stains, he looked menacing and demonic. He reeked of cheap alcohol and even cheaper tobacco. Unshaven, with greasy gray hair combed over to one side, his meager sense of vanity was exposed just like the bald spot his comb-over failed to conceal. His belly, cinched only by a piece of rope, bulged over the waistband of his overalls.

"How do you know I am a Jew?" I asked.

I was prepared to spin around, show him my rear end and slap it twice, just as Arpi had taught me to do after an incident at school had left me teary-eyed. The message was clear: that smelly old man could kiss it.

My question created quite a stir, and the noise inside the tram quickly subsided. People looked at me in silent awe. I gained control of myself, but this only encouraged the old fool even more. He was so enraged by my insolence that he didn't care what was going on around him, or what the other passengers thought of his behavior. "God damn it!" he shouted. "Do you think I'm blind? Look at your big nose. All you're missing is a pair of horns on top of your head!"

His jugular vein throbbed, his mouth exuded foul breath, and pockets of drool began to form in the corners of his lips. As my heart beat furiously, my face turned red with embarrassment and rage.

But not a single person came to my defense. The women sitting with their shopping bags simply stared out the windows, or looked down at their feet, ignoring my plight. They didn't seem to care that I was only a child. It was not that they liked this old fool, or condoned his tirade, but it wasn't worth their trouble to get involved with a drunken stranger. So I did what I had to do. I ignored him and struggled through the crowd to get to the rear door. Crying, I got off at the next stop – which wasn't even mine – and looked in the compact mirror I always carried in my school bag. Although I knew otherwise, I checked for horns on top of my head, just to be sure they hadn't started growing. I even reexamined my nose, which, while not exactly small, was not all that big either.

Crying and breathless, I ran to the kosher butcher shop on Zvonarska Street, so I wouldn't be late to meet my mother. She was bringing a chicken from the market to have it ritually slaughtered. Zvonarska St. had become the center of Jewish life in Kosice, with a kosher kitchen, a kosher butcher, and a small house of prayer, known as a *shteibel*. Inside the *shteibel* was our *cheder*, or Hebrew school, where I studied on Sundays. There were about thirty of us in the class, and our teacher, Mr. Borsky, was a kind and intelligent man who patiently taught us about our Jewish holidays and traditions. It was at the *cheder* that I finally found a group of Jewish friends who understood each other and felt safe in one another's company.

The butcher shop was housed in an L-shaped building with a storefront entrance. The butcher, Mr. Spitzer, worked only three days a week, and I was always happy to see him. He was a pious, introspective man, whose knives meant the world to him. Before slaughtering a chicken or a goose, he would thoroughly inspect the bird to make sure that it was viable for *shechita*, the Hebrew word for kosher slaughter. It was a mysterious ritual that he performed in slow motion, with his wise bespectacled face completely focused on the task at hand.

"How are you, Mr. Spitzer?" I asked timidly. "Fine, Sophia. Where is your mother?"

"I thought she would be here by now, since we had arranged to meet in the shop," I said, happy to hear his kind voice. "How do you know me?" I asked.

"I know every Jewish family in town," he said. "And I know them all by name." "Is that so? Does that nasty man from the tram know my name too?"

"They all know us," he said, smiling. "Everybody in town knows us." "So it seems," I muttered to myself.

Just then, Mother stepped into the butcher shop wearing a beautiful pink blouse and a loose brown skirt that she'd made herself. Even carrying a live chicken in her bag, she still looked elegant. I wiped away a tear and buried my face in her stomach, as she handed Mr. Spitzer the bag. "Let's begin," he said. "Let our little Sophia observe, so she can learn how it's done."

With eyes wide open, I watched and listened, determined not to miss a single detail. I knew about the laws of *kashrut*, of course, but this was the first time I had been guided through the *shechita* ritual, step by step.

"I'm not scared to watch the entire process," I boasted to Mr. Spitzer. "In Porubka, I witnessed the slaughtering of all kinds of farm animals. Chickens, geese, ducks." My mother smiled with pride.

"Here is where we differ from the Gentiles, dear Sophia," he said. "Their way of slaughtering poultry is unacceptable for us Jews. We are forbidden to eat that which is not prepared according to our laws," he said, while methodically sharpening his knives.

"What's the difference?" I asked.

"I use a special, non-serrated knife that is extremely sharp, and must be at least twice as long as the neck of the animal. I locate a particular area on the neck, look carefully, and just like that, the ritual begins."

With one quick motion of his knife, he cut the chicken's neck. There was no awkward hacking up and down, or sawing back and forth. The chicken didn't make a sound, and it did not appear to suffer in the least. It quickly bled out, and before I knew it, the whole thing was over.

"I will inspect it again to determine whether it meets our standards," Mr. Spitzer said. "Then I will remove the parts that are forbidden to be ingested, called *chelev*, and that's all there is to it. Now we can salt it, so as to extract any remaining blood, then we portion it for use, just like your mother does at home."

"But what is *chelev*?" I asked.

"Every animal contains fat and inedible parts, some more, others less. It's actually quite complicated. I'm only explaining a fraction of what I had to learn over the course of many years," he told me.

"Do you understand it now?" my mother asked. "Yes, Mother, I do!"

As we were leaving the butcher shop, Mother turned to me with a look of concern. "Aren't you late for your art class with Uncle Lajos?" she asked. By that time, I had taken several painting classes with Ludovit Feld. These sessions always lasted longer than scheduled, as he tended to get carried away, acting as though time didn't exist. He would go on and on, explaining drawing techniques, and the various methods used to measure perspective. The whole thing put me to sleep.

"I'm not going there anymore," I said, with a huff. "But why not?"

"Because I don't have the patience to sit and listen," I told Mother. "I'll go to the public art school once a week, and that's good enough."

"Do what you feel is right, but make sure you tell Uncle Lajos your decision," she admonished. "I'll do it the first chance I get," I promised Mother. But I never did.

Several months later, I went to visit Uncle Lajos to tell him the good news. I had won third prize in a children's art exhibit in Prague, and I couldn't wait to share my excitement. I remember hurrying over to his apartment to show him my award. "Look here, Uncle Lajos!" I said. "I came in third place for my picture of a cuckoo clock." I showed him the small catalog with my artwork, and my name and age printed in black ink: Sophia Manisevicova, twelve years old, student at the Public Art School in Kosice.

"Well done," he said proudly. "Keep up the good work. Now how would you like to join me for a little walk? It will do both of us some good."

"I would love to go," I replied. "But I'm afraid you're upset with me for leaving your art class." "Why would I be upset?" he said. "The most important thing is that you keep painting."

I attempted an explanation as to why I'd stopped attending his classes, but he just lifted his tiny arm, signaling to me that he understood. His genuine smile convinced me that he was being truthful.

It was a warm, sunny afternoon, and we walked together toward the brick factory, the same one where he had been years before. The Gypsies lived along this path, and not many locals ventured into this part of town. As we strolled, the Gypsy children stared at us, their mouths agape, eyes bulging in astonishment at the sight of such a tiny man walking alongside a twelve-year-old girl. Suppressing a giggle, Feld simply reached into his pocket and threw them handfuls of candy.

Meanwhile, there were problems brewing at home. I'm going for

Shachrit," my father announced early one Saturday, referring to the morning prayer service. On Friday evenings and Saturday mornings, Father always walked to the *shteibel*, where he would join the *minyan*, the group of ten men required for a Jewish prayer service. He donned his hat, put on a jacket, and collected his keys, in just that order.

"Say hello to everyone," Mother said, as she always did.

Stopping at the door, Father turned to my oldest sister. "Melanie," he said sternly. "Yes, Father?"

"You'd better stay home."

"What do you mean?" she said. "I have to meet up with friends from school. We have plans." "I don't want to hear any of your clever ideas, especially on Saturday morning when everyone else sits at home," Father said.

"Why can't I go? I don't understand. Please, please!" she pleaded.

"I know your plans because I followed you the other day," Father said. "And I saw you with *him*."

Hanka and I stood motionless. We didn't know whether to laugh or run, picturing our father spying on poor Mely. We couldn't help but wonder if he had been spying on us, too.

"Are you telling me you were following me around?" Mely asked, as tears formed in her eyes. "Yes I am," Father said. "And I caught you redhanded. I don't even want to talk about what I saw, or who I saw you with, that Duro Hornak!" he bellowed.

Melanie blushed and stared at the ground.

"My daughter was hanging around with a *goy*!" "How do you know?" Mely asked.

"Do you think I'm blind? Remember, a Jew knows every other Jew, so you'd better be careful," Father cautioned.

Melanie turned every head in town. She was well aware of her beauty, and was quite the tease.

If she happened to be crossing the tracks, the tram would come to a halt, and when she crossed the street, cars and buses did the same. But Duro didn't stand a chance. He could offer Mely all the treasures in the world, love her with his entire being, treat her like a goddess, but none of it mattered. Rule number one for Yaakov's daughters was more than clear: we could not marry outside of the faith. As much as the Jews had suffered, we had to stick together.

"This is how it is," Father said sternly. "No questions asked."

With that proclamation, he closed the door behind him, and went to pray, most probably for my sister.

Several days later, Duro Hornak paid us a visit with his parents. He appeared more than a bit distraught.

"Good afternoon," Mrs. Hornakova whispered, as she sheepishly entered our apartment.

"Do come in," Mother said. "Can I offer you some coffee?" Mother acted kind and welcoming, despite the fact that she knew what was to come.

"No, thank you," said Mr. Hornak. "We've only come to plead on our son Duro's behalf."

I felt as if I were watching a scene from *Romeo and Juliet* play out in front of my very eyes. Only instead of Verona, the setting was now Kosice, and the fair Juliet had become the fair Melanie. Mesmerized, I kept my eyes on the star-crossed lovers, and watched the drama unfold. Nobody said a word.

Finally, Mother broke the silence. "What is going on?"

Mr. Hornak stepped forward. "Our Duro is madly in love with your Melanie.

"He has threatened to take his own life if you will not allow him to marry her," the boy's mother cried.

"Melanie is free to make her own decisions. She can become Duro's wife, but she will no longer be considered our daughter," Mother replied firmly.

No more explanation was necessary. Melanie ran out of the kitchen crying. Poor Duro stood there speechless, staring off into space. He looked miserable, as though he had just endured the worst torture of his young life. The Hornaks pleaded and sobbed, but my parents wouldn't relent.

"He said he would hang himself!" Mrs. Hornakova screamed.

"Not to worry," Mother said calmly. "This will never come to pass." There was not a hint of hesitation in her voice. She never doubted Duro's longevity, or Mely's Jewish future.

As I absorbed the whole scene, I realized that my parents' decision directly affected my future, as well as my sister Hanka's. At the age of twelve, I didn't know much about matters of the heart, but days earlier, while cleaning our bedroom, I had come across Hanka's diary. I was impressed by how she had described her suitors down to the finest detail. The following day, I foolishly admitted my snooping, and asked my sister where she hid that magnet that attracted all those boys. She was irate at my indiscretion, and didn't speak to me for the rest of the afternoon. I never snooped again, and she never did tell me where she hid that magnet.

Defeated, the Hornaks solemnly left our house. The scene that followed was brief, but it made a lasting impression. My sisters and I lined up in order of size; Melanie, Hanka, and then I stood in front of our parents, who did not seem upset or angry in the least. We stood speechless, waiting for what would come next. Father postured a bit, took a deep breath, and then said from the depths of his being, "No daughters of Yaakov Manisevic will ever marry someone who is not Jewish. Is this clear?"

The three of us nodded our heads in silent agreement.

"It is either them or us," he said. "I don't ever want to see one of my daughters carousing with a *goy* again!"

I felt numb and could only continue to nod my head.

Next, Mother stepped into the fray. "It is up to you," she said. "But if any of you brings a non-Jew into this household, you can pack your bags and forget where you came from."

I got the message loud and clear. It felt as if her words took on a life of their own, and floated above the kitchen cabinets, where, one by one, they calmly descended and engraved themselves into my heart and memory.

"If you do, we will sit *Shiva* for you for a week, cover all the mirrors, sit on the floor and solemnly mourn," Mother said. "That is what we do when someone dies."

I stood there stunned, trying to make sense of her words. Who will I choose? I wondered. I knew almost all of the Jewish boys in town, and my pickings were slim, to say the least. And what about Melanie and Duro? Was it really that easy to fall out of love? What about Hanka and her magnet? Was it possible to program it to attract only Jewish men? Luckily, I was the youngest of the three, and had plenty of time to find the answers to my questions. But I was already thinking how I could avoid such a fate as my oldest sister's.

Right then and there, in the corner of our kitchen on Czechoslovakian Army Street, I determined to remain a proud Jew, in spirit and form, for all the days of my life. Watching that awful scene unfold in our kitchen, something within me had shifted. I remember it so clearly; it was as if the flower of my heart had opened, and I could finally see the beauty of who I truly was.

Before the year was out, Melanie followed my parents' wishes and married a nice Jewish boy. I was thirteen at the time, and Melanie was 21, but to me she seemed like such a grown woman. In her wedding dress and high-heeled shoes, she made a gorgeous bride. Her new husband Jindra was from Prague, and had come to Kosice to work in the printing factory. With my parents proudly looking on, they were married under the *chuppa*, the wedding canopy, in our small *shteibel* on Zvonarska Street.

Melanie Manisevicova had now become Mrs. Melanie Friedmanova.

Time flew by, and only Hanka and I remained at home. By now we were both in high school, and we knew that sooner or later it would be Hanka's turn to marry. At an evening dance held at Buzna, an old synagogue that had been transformed into Kosice's cultural center, a handsome young man approached my sister and asked if she'd like to dance. His name was Bandi Stark, and like us, he attended High Holiday services at the large Orthodox synagogue on Pushkinova Street. Hanka had noticed him before and gladly accepted his invitation.

On Rosh Hashana, the Jewish New Year, and Yom Kippur, the Day of Atonement that comes ten days later, the synagogue would be bursting at the seams. Inside, men and women would be separated, with women seated upstairs. This gave us a fantastic vantage point for checking out all the boys down below. Whenever one of us spotted a cute guy, Hanka and I would poke each other, then nod in agreement, trying not to giggle. We looked forward to the High Holidays, and took great pleasure in our balcony seats, even though under the Communist regime, attending any kind of religious service was strictly forbidden.

Bandi was a strapping athletic guy who attended the Technical University in the city. He was also an accomplished soccer player and top referee in the national league. But most importantly, he was a real *mensch*. After that first, fateful dance, Bandi and Hanka's courtship blossomed, and they dated for nearly two years. One night at the Carpano Restaurant, a famous eatery on Main Street, Bandi proposed. Naturally, Hanka accepted. They still have the two Cinzano glasses they stole from the bar, after they shared their first engagement drink. The following Shabbat, Hanka giggled and smiled throughout the entire meal. She could not contain her excitement at the dinner table.

"I think somebody wants to tell us something," Mother said, with a sly smile. "Not me!" I screamed.

"Me neither," Hanka muttered, blushing. "Really?" Mother said.

Now that she was the center of attention, Hanka nonchalantly moved her left hand from underneath the table and there, on her ring finger, was a shiny, gold engagement band. She waved her hand around, laughing and shrieking with joy.

"I'm engaged!" she blurted.

"What?" I said, trying to digest the news. But I was the only one who registered shock. My parents had already heard the good news through the grapevine. It's amazing how fast news can travel, especially in a small town like Kosice. I'm not sure whether it was the fact that everyone knew everybody else's business, or that people routinely spied on one another, but in any case, nothing could remain secret for very long.

"*Mazel Tov!*" said Father, as he raised his glass to Hanka and Bandi's future. Just as with Melanie, our parents' rules had been obeyed, and all parties were satisfied.

Was he a Jew? Yes.

Wedding under the *chuppa*? Yes. Parents? Ecstatic.

Newlyweds? Madly in love.

Now, at last, it was my turn. Would I follow the same trend as my sisters and marry within the faith? I traveled back in time all the way to Porubka, by the water well where I had played with a pail and shovel as a child, munching on a piece of potato candy. This sweet and affordable delight, made of potato starch, came in a few different colors, and my all-time favorite was pink. With my little shovel and pail in hand, I would dig away at a hole, as if I could create a passageway that would lead straight from Porubka to America, the land I knew only in my dreams. In America, the land of opportunity, I would be free to be a Jew holding my head high, with joy in my heart, and a new light sparkling in my eyes.

I was done dreaming my dream. Now I was ready to live it. Yes, I wanted to marry a Jew. But most of all, I wanted the freedom to make my own choice, and I wanted to marry for love.

CHAPTER SEVEN

֍

Dreaming of Love and Escape

Kosice, After 1968

I N 1968, WARSAW PACT troops invaded Czechoslovakia, crushing the
democratic reform movement and turning the clock backwards. Now
the world was divided into two hostile camps: the capitalists, a world
of imperialist enemies, and the socialists, who had promised us greater
freedom, but only clamped down harder. Things got much worse. The
shops were empty, and a sense of fear and foreboding lurked in the shad-
ows of everyday life. Generally speaking, we were afraid of everything.

The practice of religion was strictly forbidden, leaving people to attend
their churches, as well as the few remaining synagogues, in secret. Our
Jewish community had dwindled to a fraction of its former size, since
those who could afford to, quickly fled the country. As a result, our beloved *cheder* had to close its doors. Carrying only one suitcase, determined
to build a better life, entire families emigrated to America, Israel, Canada,
Australia, or Western Europe. At the tender age of fourteen, how I wished
I could be one of them.

The late sixties were a time of paranoia and suspicion. People met secretly at each other's homes, debating conspiracy theories, plotting their
escapes, and glancing over their shoulders as though someone might be
spying on them. All of the socialist freedoms we had been promised only
made us prisoners again, but in a different way. Slowly but surely, my
parents had gotten used to life in Kosice, and my mother had abandoned
her dream of emigrating to America. That little flame of hope she had
carried for so long was finally extinguished. She knew that my father's

stubbornness would lead them nowhere, but at the same time, she would never leave without him. I was the only one who remained committed to the dream, and I prayed with all my heart that it would soon come true.

At that time, I was studying to become a pharmaceutical technician at City Medical High School on Moyzesova Street. Zoya Timkova, whom I nicknamed Timka, was my best friend. The girls in my class no longer considered one's religion to be the most important factor in determining friendships, but a few of them still rejected me when they learned of my background. Generally speaking, though, they were more concerned with how they looked and what to wear, just like teenagers all over the world.

Disco fever had hit Kosice, and whether it was the alleged hot Gypsy blood coursing through my veins, or the hotter Jewish side of me, I simply loved to dance.

Without fail, I was always the first one on the dance floor. Timka, my friend Helga (whom I'd known since elementary school) and I, would spend the entire week discussing our outfits, how to accessorize them, and which way to style our hair for the coming Saturday. We eagerly awaited each appointed dance night and would spend hours preparing to show up at the V Club, the most popular disco in town. At the club, we would strut around holding hands, blushing, and dreaming of falling madly in love on the dance floor.

I must confess that, at times, I envied my friends. I was the only Jew among them, and when it came to choosing a mate, I didn't have the same options. It made me nervous to think that my chosen one absolutely *had* to be Jewish, and the anxiety only festered when the Jewish boys I did meet didn't make my heart sing. Then one day, my worst fears came true. I fell in love with a *goy*.

Martin was a psychology student with dirty blond hair and dreamy eyes. He had a beautiful smile that stretched from one ear to the other, and he knew how to make me laugh. I enjoyed spending time with him, but I also knew from the start that our relationship was doomed and we were both bound to suffer greatly. I could just imagine his parents sitting in our kitchen, playing out the very same scene from *Romeo & Juliet* that I had witnessed with my sister. The thought of it made my stomach turn.

But erasing Martin from my mind was much easier said than done.

In addition to my mother's personality, I had also inherited her sense of style and her eye for detail. Thanks to her influence, I adored beautiful, well-made clothes, especially when I was the one wearing them. We had a sewing machine at home, and from the time we were little girls, Mother would make us lovely dresses. She took great pride in our appearance, and every piece of clothing had to be perfectly sewn, inside and out.

Our most prized possessions, and our conduit to the world of fashion, were our two-inch thick German department store catalogs, *Neckerman* and *Quelle*. Another catalog, *Burda*, included patterns, which made it easy to copy the very clothes I saw in its pages. Many a night, I would take the catalogs to bed with me, flipping through the pages, poring over every image that caught my eye. I knew I could never have such beautiful clothes, trapped as I was behind the invisible, yet ever-present Iron Curtain, but by studying these pages, I taught myself how to replicate them.

At first I sewed only for myself, but pretty soon, I also began sewing for friends. I made hip- hugger pants, with the zippers sewn on the front, rather than the side. This was quite rebellious, as Mother forbade us from wearing zippers in the front. But what she considered provocative, I considered stylish. Word of my skill quickly spread through Kosice, and before long, I had paying customers lining up at the door. My pants became so popular that I was able to open my own business, while still in high school. I accepted bribes in the form of chocolate, books, or extra cash, which enabled my customers to skip the waiting list. Soon enough, I expanded my repertoire, sewing dresses, skirts, and blouses, often without relying on a pattern.

With the money I made from sales, I would replenish my supplies. It was not uncommon for me to purchase fabric in the morning, then show off my latest designs that very same evening. My friends, especially my best friend, Timka, wanted nothing more than to be seen wearing a pair of my pin-striped or checkerboard pants.

"When are you going to make me a new pair?" she asked one morning. The weather was nice, and we were picking four-leaf clovers in the small park on Moyzesova St.

"You're going to have to wait," I told her. "I'm very busy these days."

"But who is more important than your own best friend?" Timka implored. "Who in the world could possibly come before *me*, the best possible person to show off your beautifully-sewn pants?"

"Those young actors from the City Group Theater," I replied.

"Are you serious?" she said. "I *must* have a new pair of pants for my date. I really like this new guy."

"Okay," I promised. "I'll do my best."

But before I could say another word, my eyes fell on a four-leaf clover. "It's an omen of love," Timka said, smiling. "I can feel it in the air." Her words made me blush.

"Tell me everything," she said.

"Where do I begin? I don't know what to do," I told her. "I could really use some good, sound advice right now."

"I don't know what to say, as it's never been an issue for me," Timka said. "I really don't understand this way of thinking. If you want to be with someone, why is it so important that he be of the same faith?"

"Because it is," was my only answer.

"Is there something you're not telling me? You look so worried all the time."

"You know my parents, Timka, and you know that they will never approve of Martin. I feel like I'm living a double life," I confessed.

"What do you mean?"

"Let's just leave it at that," I huffed.

I was not in the mood to dwell on the details of Father's number one rule, but at the same time, I couldn't erase Martin from my heart and mind. However, while I appeared normal on the surface, a volcano was waiting to erupt inside of me. Although things seemed hopeless at times, I continued to plot my escape. I spent my days at school with Timka, weekends sewing with Helga, and afternoons apprenticing at the pharmacy on Marathon Square with Laura, an old friend who had already earned her Master's degree, and was a practicing pharmacist. We'd met at the *cheder* many years before and always looked forward to spending time together, dreaming of our futures.

When summer came, Timka and I would go out to gossip and flirt. "Are we going to the film festival?" I asked Timka one afternoon. "Absolutely," she said. "I wouldn't miss it for the world."

For one week every summer, Kosice hosted the "Film Festival for the Working Class." The festival played Communist propaganda films, including tributes to the Russian Army, but lucky for us, it also screened foreign films. That year the main feature was *Midnight Cowboy* and we couldn't wait to see it.

"Let's meet at the Basta Club before we go to the festival," Timka said.

"And what about Martin?" I asked. "Is he coming?" Timka had become our secret liaison, which meant that she knew more about his plans than I did.

"Without a doubt," she said. "I ran into him today on Leninova Street, in front of the festival billboards. It's all arranged. All you have to do is come up with an excuse so that your parents will let you go."

"You're amazing," I said, and winked.

"You should see how beautiful the billboards look," Timka said. "Maximillian Bush did a wonderful job."

Maximillian Finsterbush was a scenic painter for the City Theater who had shortened his last name to Bush after the war. As the official artist for the Kosice Film Festival, he was responsible for painting all of the promotional billboards, which were displayed in public parks. Our families were related and would frequently visit together. Maximillian's wife Irenka, who we had nicknamed Manci, was a one-of-a-kind woman. I loved it when she spoke her unique blend of Hungarian and Slovakian, and how she endearingly referred to her husband as "my Bushinko." I had never seen Manci without a freshly styled hairdo and heavy pink lipstick, which she wore on her teeth as much as on her lips. I enjoyed our visits, and would often help her tidy up the house or take out the garbage. At festival time, she always had free tickets waiting for me.

I had met Bushinko a few times at Ludovit Feld's art studio. They were good friends, and Bushinko would visit the little giant from time to time. On occasion, I ventured to Feld's studio, only to find Bushinko sitting silently, or gently inquiring as to how Feld was feeling. After the war, when Uncle Lajos returned to Kosice, Bushinko shared his studio with him, until he was able to find his own. As a token of appreciation, Feld gave Bushinko two original drawings, both of which captured the atrocities of the Holocaust.

It took clever planning, as well as subversive help from friends, for Martin and me to spend time together. Luckily, I had Laura's younger brother, Marian Berger, as a willing decoy. In addition to his good looks and charm, Marian was also Jewish, which made him the perfect foil for my parents. In order to trick them into thinking he was taking me out, Marian would pick me up at the door. If it wasn't one Berger, it was another, as Laura would also drop by to bring my mother prescription medications, saving her the trouble of waiting in endless lines.

Our two families were fond of each other, and Mother wanted more than anything for me to develop a relationship with Marian. In an effort to lure him, she would buy me the latest fashions. Marian's father felt the same way about me. In our Jewish parents' dreams, they were already dancing at our wedding, celebrating the bar and bat mitzvahs of their many grandchildren to come. My relationship with Marian proved convenient for both of us, as he was always busy, studying or hanging out with friends. This allowed me to spend more time with Martin. Officially, I was involved with a boy my parents approved of, but secretly, I was very much in love with a *goy*.

When we met at the Basta Club, a private club housed in the basement of an apartment building, we found Robert, Timka's new discovery, and Martin, my dear *goy*, waiting for us at the bar.

"What would you ladies like to drink?" they asked.

"I'll take a glass of Midnight America," I blurted, and proceeded to gulp down a beer. "Guys, let's go before Sophia actually moves there!" Timka said.

She dragged us out of the club, and we sped off to the amphitheater. It was a beautiful, summer night, and the outdoor cinema was packed with young Socialist Union members and their Communist parents. Watching *Midnight Cowboy*, we could see the "evil" world of the rotten capitalists with our very own eyes. But instead of being horrified, I was mesmerized. I loved watching Jon Voight, the Midnight Cowboy, stroll the streets of New York City, looking lost and disillusioned among a sea of towering skyscrapers. How I longed for that same freedom.

As well as I knew that my name was Sophia, I knew that one day I would make it to America. I refused to let the Communists and their narrow worldview ruin my life, and I refused to become another ordinary, middle-class woman, digesting their propaganda on a daily basis. As the movie went on, I stopped looking at the subtitles, and paid less and less attention to the plot. I soon began to picture myself standing beside the Midnight Cowboy, as he boarded his bus to freedom, en route to New York City. Right then and there, I closed my eyes, and imagined myself free. Only instead of a free cowboy, I was a free Jew.

As Timka waved goodbye, she looked back over her shoulder and winked.

"Will I see you at the flea market tomorrow morning?" I asked, winking back. "We have a lot of clothes to sell. Try not to be late."

"Stop worrying, I'll be there!" Timka said.

Timka and I had started selling our old clothes at the city's flea market. We would gather skirts, pants, and blouses that we no longer wore, wash and iron them, then sell them for a profit.

"So, how did you like the movie?" Martin asked, as we left the amphitheater. "Oh, I just loved it!" I exclaimed.

"You're going to leave me one day, aren't you?" he said out of the blue. "While you were watching the movie, I was watching you."

"Martin . . ." But I could say no more, as he covered my lips with his. A strange sensation rippled through my body, not because of his kiss, but because of the thought that one day, I would make my American dream come true.

"Let's go before someone sees us," I said, and quickly changed the subject.

When we returned to the Basta club to meet up with our friends, the theme song from *Midnight Cowboy*, "Everybody's Talkin'," was still playing in my head. People were talking, but I couldn't hear a word they were saying. It was at that very moment that I knew that I was "going where the sun is shining, through the pouring rain, skipping over the ocean like a stone." I didn't know how, I didn't know when, but I knew I would live there, in America.

That same night, I also realized that my relationship with Martin was over.

꫞

CHAPTER EIGHT

Attempting to Escape

Kosice, Prague, Cheb, After 1968

I T WAS A GLORIOUS, sunny day at the flea market, and the crowds filtered in. On the surface, everything looked fine and life went on as usual. But on the inside, I could feel myself about to explode.

"I'll miss you," Timka said, as if she could read my thoughts.

"Why not come with me?" I asked, as I packed our unsold clothes into a suitcase. "Do you really feel that escape is your only option?" Timka asked, nearly crying. "I'm suffocating here," I said.

"You're exaggerating," she countered. "Is it really that difficult?"

"If only you could walk in my shoes, even for a day, maybe you would understand. I just can't stay here anymore. I have no desire to marry a single one of the boys that my parents approve of, give birth to a bunch of kids, and live the exact same life as my mother."

"I can't wait to get married!" Timka squealed. "Robert is the man for me, and did I mention that his mother is also Jewish?"

"You don't say? If they reveal their identities, you can impress them all with your knowledge of Jewish tradition. Theoretically, your Robert is Jewish too, since it's passed down through the mother's blood line."

"Don't be a fool!" Timka pleaded. "Stay here. Please don't leave me behind!" "If I stay here, I'll go mad."

"But you will still be around for my wedding, won't you?"

Timka and Robert Molnar, her ski instructor from Banska Bystrica, were deeply in love. In wintertime he gave her skiing lessons, and they were a perfect match.

"You must hurry then, if you want me to dance at your wedding. I've already submitted my application for a Swiss visa."

"What? Why Switzerland?" she asked. "Because I must get to Zurich."

"Well, Sophia, it's not me that has to do the hurrying, it's you. I just found out that I'm pregnant."

"Timka!" I squealed with delight. "It's true."

"*Mazel tov*," I said, and hugged my best friend.

"Look," she said, pointing at her stomach. "I'm carrying a half-Jew under my heart." "Does that mean you are only half pregnant?" I joked.

"I'll be moving with him to Banska Bystrica, but you, Sophia, I'm confused as to why you are choosing Zurich. I thought you wanted to go America?"

"Zurich is only a stopover. I'm told that I can find the International Red Cross there. First I have to register, declare that I'm Jewish, and then they'll help me attain political asylum in America."

"I'm concerned for you, Sophia. I don't think you should tell a soul. You know how envious people can be. Some are just plain jealous, and they'll try to thwart your success. I'll keep my fingers crossed, since you don't speak their language, and have never been to Western Europe. Just think it through carefully before you proceed any further," she begged of me.

"Timka, you can't imagine how hard it is for me to keep all this inside. Don't worry, the only ones that know beside my family are my most trusted friends. I am going straight to Chicago to stay with my Aunt Blanca. She has promised to help me out."

"What about your mother?" Timka asked.

"What about her? She can't stop crying, and the thought of not seeing me again is keeping her awake at night, but she knows my mind is made up. She even offered me $200 to help me get started. I've already exchanged our local currency for $60, the maximum we're allowed to leave with. I've also paid for my visa and somehow managed to get contacts that might be able to help me once I arrive in Zurich."

"For God's sake, Sophia, you don't know a soul there."

"Don't worry about me, Timka. I sewed my gold chain with the Star of David inside the belt on my dress, so that nobody can find it. The moment I cross that border will be the moment I put it on and never take it off again. It was my bat mitzvah present, and I have faith that it will always protect me.

My mind is made up."

"Are you sure?" she asked, her eyes begging.

"I'm going! And I'm not even upset anymore that I didn't get into the university, despite the fact that I passed the exam with flying colors. You were right, Timka. Even my lucky talisman, my Star of David, didn't have the power to create one more opening for a Jew."

"I can't argue with you," Timka said. "It looks like you've already made up your mind, and have everything figured out. Will we ever see each other again?"

"Honestly, Timka, I don't know. But I do have faith that the day will come." Timka stepped toward me and offered her hand.

"Take care of yourself," I said.

I kissed my best friend on the cheek, and gently rubbed her expanding belly. "You too," she said, and we embraced for what might be the last time.

After graduating from high school, I kept making pants on the side, and landed a job in the city's Department of Health, where I warmed up a beat-up, old office chair. Punching my time card was my grandiose entrance into the working world. At the same time, my parents were begging me to find a suitable Jewish bachelor, so I could follow in my sisters' footsteps. But after breaking up with Martin, I was no longer interested in a relationship. I knew it would only serve as an unnecessary diversion.

The totalitarian regime had me in its grip, and instead of openly attending synagogue services, I was forced, like everyone else, to attend meetings of the Socialist Union Youth Group and the Revolutionary Union Movement. I refused to speak openly, as one never knew who was listening. In those days, even the walls had ears.

As I wove a web of deception around the system and my parents, I could no longer bear to deceive myself. I began to plot my escape, and would sometimes even drop hints to my friends. "I might not be staying in town much longer," I'd say, casually referencing my departure. The thought of living in America so excited me that I threw all caution to the wind. For years I had been secretly plotting my escape. Ever since I was a little girl, digging a hole with my pail and shovel beside the water well in Porubka, I had pictured this moment. Nothing else mattered now except for my exodus. This wasn't just the whim of a new high school graduate, it was my calling, my life's purpose. I believed I could conquer the world.

The only thing that weighed heavily on my conscience was the thought of leaving behind my parents, my sisters, and our home. I knew full well that I might never see them again. But I could no longer imagine myself as an ordinary, middle-class citizen, accepting the propaganda we were spoon-fed three times a day, after every meal. I could no longer climb up the invisible ladder of socialist success, marching in the annual May Day parade, or carrying a fresh bouquet of tulips for International Women's Day in March. Each night, I fell asleep with visions of skyscrapers in my head. Until finally I packed my entire life into one suitcase and waited impatiently for the day when I could follow my lucky star.

At home it was another story. Mother and Father hugged me for what seemed like an eternity, as though they wanted to hold on for just a moment longer. When D-day finally arrived, I begged them not to come to the train station with me, as I didn't want to attract any unwanted attention. But my parents were unyielding, and they insisted on seeing me off.

"Mother, I am finally leaving the Iron Curtain for good," I said, standing on the tracks. "I am off to a new world to seek freedom. I promise to contact you as soon as possible." I was trying to reassure myself, as well as her.

"Take good care of yourself and remember, we love you always," Mother said.

She and I cried together, while Father stood by, unhappy to see me leave, but knowing full well that I could not be stopped. I kissed them both and then boarded the train. As I waved through the window, I watched their contours disappear in the distance. I had a berth in the sleeper car, although I can't say I got very much sleep. Thanks to the excitement coursing through my veins, I couldn't keep my eyes closed. The next morning, we pulled into Prague.

The following night I had a connecting train to Zurich, via Stuttgart, which would take me to my new world of freedom. I spent the afternoon meandering around the streets of the "hundred towered" city like a zombie. I'd barely slept the night before. I felt so numb that I didn't even notice the famous Horologe Tower rising up in the Old City Square. In order to avoid any unwanted attention from the ever-present secret police, I visited Mely's mother-in-law's apartment. I stopped over for more hugs, goodbyes, and blessings, and then boarded the next train toward my destiny.

In my train compartment were two Czech women married to Germans, and a Slovak woman who was a tourist, just like me. All of them appeared to be seasoned travelers, and I knew they could sense what was happening. My heart was beating so fast, it must have been obvious that I was scared. "If there is anything you would like us to help you with, or hold on to, so you won't have to hide it from the customs officers, we can do that for you," one of the women offered.

"I have nothing to hide," I replied.

I started to think about the $200 I had sewn into the belt of my dress, and the Star of David sewn beside it. How I envied these women for their easy lives. They smelled so good, and looked so relaxed. I wanted such a life for myself, but without the German husbands, of course. That would surely finish my mother off for good, as, after her experience during the Holocaust, she couldn't bear to hear the sound of people speaking German.

When the train came to a halt at the Czech-German border in Cheb, I felt as if my blood had stopped circulating. "Good day," the Czech border officer announced, as he entered our car. "Your passports, visas and custom declaration forms, please."

To my surprise, everything went smoothly. The train began to move, and we headed towards the German border. A few minutes later, the train stopped again, and we were asked to follow the same procedure. But this time it was the German border officers who ran the show. They checked our papers, stamped and returned our passports, and wished us a safe trip.

I'd done it!

The train sat on the tracks for a good ten minutes, before the car door opened, and two officers in long trench coats looked us up and down. "Is one of you Comrade Manisevicova?" the officer asked.

"That is me," I said, looking straight into his face.

In that split second, I knew that my journey was over. The two Czech-German women gave me sad looks. I felt as if I'd transformed from a tourist back into an inmate in my Communist prison, right in front of their eyes.

"Gather you belongings, you are coming with us," one of the officers commanded. "Why? What is the matter?" I asked innocently.

"We just need to verify some information." "What about my train?"

"Don't worry, it will be here waiting for you," he said, smirking.

While I collected my belongings, they stood over me, watching my every move. I silently thanked God that I didn't give my $200 to those

Czech-German women, since it would have been impossible to retrieve. I could tell from the way they nodded and looked me in the eyes, that they felt sympathy for my plight.

It was a warm July night, around 4 a.m., and the sun had not yet risen. Shaking all over, I followed the officers off the train. As soon as we disembarked, my train to freedom took off without me. I stood there silently watching it disappear, just as my parents had watched my train to Prague fade into the distance.

"Your passport," an officer yelled, as soon as we arrived at the border police station. "Excuse me?"

"Comrade Manisevicova, your passport!" "What did I do?" I asked nervously. "Your passport!" he screamed again. "Here," I said, as I handed it over.

My head was spinning with questions I could not answer. What is going to happen to me? What am I going to do? Where will I end up? What was next? I could just imagine my mother, already a nervous wreck, fainting on the kitchen floor. Gathering my wits, I asked for permission to use the restroom. While inside, I shredded all my foreign contact names and addresses from my notebook, flushed them down the toilet three times, then returned to my captors.

Those officers eyed me like a criminal. I sat there for hours, and nobody said a word. Nobody so much as offered me a glass of water. Finally, by late morning, the taller of the two officers walked over to me. "Comrade Manisevicova, we are confiscating your passport," he said. "It is no longer your property. Your trip is not in accordance with the rules of Socialist Government. You attempted to defect. You must return to your home immediately."

"There must be some kind of misunderstanding," I said.

He said no more; he just pointed to the doors. As I stepped forward and made my way to the exit, I could feel the other officers' eyes boring through me. For them, it was all over. They never even bothered to inform me why they had revoked my papers, or how they reached their conclusion. As was typical of the thugs who so blindly served their Communist masters, all they wanted was to see my fear. They represented State security, but in truth, they were more lawless than law-abiding.

The taller officer appeared to smile. He looked rather dapper in his uniform, but still, he had the look of a snitch. He was handsome, all right, with watery green eyes and a thin mustache. Judging from his expression and ironic smirk, I suspected that they had been trailing me for some time. Had someone ratted me out? Who could it have been? Who needed a promotion on my account? What would happen at work? What was to become of me? I imagined myself back in Kosice, most likely jobless, if this border drama came back to haunt me. My biggest fear was that people would lose their interest, and I'd have nowhere to turn. In such a provincial city as Kosice, bad news traveled fast. Searching my soul for answers, I wondered who would do such a thing.

In that instant, I lost my faith in everything and everyone. I had no passport and no money. It was only me, awkwardly dragging my suitcase through the deserted German Czech border crossing at Cheb. As I broke into a cold sweat, I could feel the goose bumps popping up across my skin. This happened despite the fact that the temperature was pushing 90 degrees. My mouth felt bitterly dry, and it seemed as though my life had ceased to be my own. The Iron Curtain had slapped me directly in the face, and I was horribly bruised. Once again, I had been locked up behind those invisible, iron bars.

As I walked over countless railroad tracks, dragging my luggage, I looked neither left nor right. I just stared at the ground. In the filthy mirror at the train station bathroom, I barely recognized myself.

While washing my hands in that wretched bathroom sink, the two blisters I developed while dragging my luggage started to bleed. I was starving, and my shrunken stomach made sure I was aware of it and wouldn't stop rumbling.

I had just enough money to get back to Prague, but not enough to make it home to Kosice.

According to government rules, we were forbidden from carrying Czechoslovakian currency, as well as any form of identification other than a passport. For the second time, my sister Mely's mother-in-law came to my rescue. Without any comment, she loaned me money for airfare, so that I could arrive home safe and sound. In the meantime, she reassured me that she would contact my parents. "Good luck, my dear," she said kindly, and showed me to the door.

"Go, just go," she said, as I leaned in to kiss her good-bye.

Nobody knew whether or not I was being followed, and I became so paranoid that all I could see were secret agents and traitors in the faces of those who passed me on the street. Clutching my borrowed airfare money in my hand, I thought, "At least I'll get home safely." The last thing I expected was for another drama to unfold.

"Your travel documents, please," an officer demanded.

I shrugged my shoulders and calmly said, "I don't have any. My passport has been confiscated by your colleagues at Cheb this morning. As you know, I am not allowed to carry another form of ID while traveling abroad."

"Well then, Comrade, we cannot let you board the plane without your passport."

"I just want to go home," I cried through hot, bitter tears. "I already explained to you that my passport was confiscated earlier this morning."

"Your name?" he barked. "Sophia Manisevicova." "Address?"

"The Czechoslovakian Army Street, Kosice." "Who do you live with?"

"My parents."

"Their names?"

"Simone and Yaakov Manisevic."

"That's enough. Wait here, while we check your identity." With that, he turned on his heel and walked away.

An hour later, the officer returned and allowed me to board the plane. But in the meantime, my fellow passengers had been staring at me like I was a serial killer. I could only assume that because of my name, the officers had figured out that I was Jewish, and wanted to defect. Sitting in a window seat, I said goodbye to Prague's skyline, as if for the last time. Two hours later, we made a smooth landing in the Kosice airport. Nobody was waiting for me at the gate. Braving the commotion of travelers hugging their dear ones hello and goodbye, I stepped alone into the warm, sunny day. I had returned home to my prison.

CHAPTER NINE

෫

Playing it Safe

Czechoslovakia, 1970s

THE SUMMER OF 1974 was the worst summer of my life so far. Sentenced to living back in Kosice, I joined the ranks of the Socialist collective, and began playing it safe. Fortunately for me, nobody found out about the border incident. I returned to my job at the City Department of Health as if nothing had happened, and for eight hours a day I pushed papers and warmed the same beat-up old office chair.

Back at home the atmosphere grew tense. As a young woman with no serious prospects for a partner and my future unclear, I felt trapped. My parents, believing that time was rapidly running out, were anxious to see me in the arms of a prospective suitor. I could also sense that deep down inside, they were relieved that my escape plan had failed.

In addition to Mother's concerns about her youngest daughter becoming a spinster, she was also distressed by the unannounced visits of the secret police and the interrogations that followed my botched attempt. The policemen were not dressed in official uniforms, but because of her experiences at Auschwitz, anyone in a position of authority had the power to make her tremble.

One Saturday morning, my father volunteered to install a new roof over the *mikvah*, the Jewish ritual bath where married women went to purify themselves. Mother pleaded with him not to do this work on the Sabbath, but he didn't listen. Father marched out the door and headed straight to the small structure on Zvonarska Street, where he climbed up a ladder and set to work.

Several hours later, the phone rang. Mother answered and heard the voice of Mr. Klein, the elderly caretaker of our little *shteibel*, who told her that Father had fallen off the roof. Mr. Klein had found him lying unconscious. I watched Mother's face grow paler by the second, as the caretaker spoke. "I'll be right there," she said quietly, and placed the receiver back in its cradle. "What happened?" I asked. Part of me didn't want to hear the answer.

"Your father fell off the roof," Mother said. "Let's hurry. Someone has already called for an ambulance, and we must arrive first."

Mother had never learned how to drive, so we ran down the street in desperation, sticking out our thumbs hoping that someone would stop and offer us a ride. As we ran along those familiar streets, minutes felt like hours. We arrived at the scene just as the ambulance pulled up to the curb. The paramedics lifted my father off the ground, placed him on a stretcher, and slid him into the ambulance. We jumped in beside him and made our way to the hospital, sirens blaring. The doctor delivered the bad news in person. Father had broken his coccyx bone and suffered numerous pelvic fractures. The prognosis was not good. He might never be able to walk again.

After six weeks in the hospital, Father finally came home, and he vowed to never again so much as lift a finger on Shabbat, our day of rest. He believed that while his intentions were good, God had punished him just the same. Father spent nearly the whole summer laid up, and we were all anxious to see whether he would recuperate. Thankfully, through intense rehabilitation and a strong will, Father was able to stand up. Slowly but surely, at first relying on a cane, he relearned how to walk. He also kept his promise and never again worked on a Saturday.

Timka had by now moved with Robert Molnar, her new husband, to Banska Bystrica, a city in Central Slovakia. While she was expecting her firstborn child, we kept in touch by phone. My friend Laura Berger, the pharmacist, was in deep trouble with her father for dating a non-Jew. Just as it was with my father, Laura's father could not bear the thought of his daughter marrying a *goy*. While Laura spent more and more time with her new beau, her father tried everything in his power to break them up. The relationship seemed serious though, and I feared that Laura might get married without her family's blessing. I didn't want to see her disowned forever.

Mr. Berger, a widower, had different plans for his daughter and two sons. He had always liked me, and considered me a suitable match for Marian. Just as my mother had done earlier, he tried to take my friendship with his son to the next level. He would tell Marian to visit me at work and bring me bouquets of fresh flowers, looking dapper and freshly shaven. Like any parent, all Mr. Berger wanted was for his children to be happy. Since he was a widower, he took full responsibility for raising them, and he hoped that this time the *shidduch*, or arranged marriage, would work out. But for all of Mr. Berger's hard work, it was not meant to be. Marian was nothing more than a red herring, a diversion as I planned my second escape attempt.

Marian and I continued with our charade for the rest of the summer, and I even went so far as to announce our engagement. By that time, I was completely disgusted with the entire city, the Communist regime, socialism, and the bored, tired faces of my comrades, who always seemed to turn to the bottle for relief. I was genuinely miserable. As the days stretched on, I shut down. I felt as though every cell in my body had gone on strike. Thank God for my feisty, rebellious spirit, because had I been weak, I would have given up my dream long ago. But I would not allow them to win.

Mr. Berger was relentless in his efforts to end the love affair between Laura and her non-Jewish boyfriend. After using every tool at his disposal, he finally managed to convince her to visit some relatives in Brooklyn for two weeks. Mr. Berger went to great lengths to obtain the necessary documentation to send his daughter to America, far away from her non-Jewish boyfriend. But he lost her forever, because she never returned home.

I, on the other hand, was still close to my father. Before the High Holidays in the fall, as was the custom, Father traveled to the cemetery in Porubka to visit his father's grave. I had never visited my grandfather's grave, and I begged Father to take me along.

"Let her go with you," Mother said. "It would put me at ease to know that you are not alone.

After all, you still haven't fully recovered."

Father was not a youngster, and his accident took quite a toll on his health – not to mention Mother's nerves.

"Stop exaggerating, Simone. I am still capable and strong," he said, only half-joking. Then he turned toward me and smiled. "I must say, Sophia, it makes me very happy to know that you would like to share this experience with me."

As father put on his cap, kissed Mother goodbye, and grabbed his keys, I smiled back. Driving past the farms and villages, Father and I made small talk. But as we neared our destination, his face suddenly turned serious.

"Sophia, do you realize that the time has arrived for you to find someone to spend the rest of your life with?" he asked, tightening his grip on the steering wheel.

"Unfortunately, the boys I like are already taken, and as for the others, well . . ." I said, my voice trailing off.

"Somehow I knew it would be difficult with you," he mumbled, as he shook his head. "Besides, you know I don't want to spend the rest of my life here," I said. "One unsuccessful attempt will not stop me."

"What are you talking about?" He looked puzzled. "I still want to leave," I said.

"Perhaps it is not in the stars for you. Get your head out of the clouds, stay focused on what is around you, and find someone who makes you happy. Your mother will never find any peace until she sees that you are being taken care of."

That, of course, meant being married. "I understand," I said.

We sat in silence until finally Father spoke again.

"Last Friday evening at shul, a man approached me," he said.

"So what?"

"His name is Mr. Newman. He is originally from the city of Brno, in Moravia. His whole family moved to Caracas, Venezuela, and they are quite well off."

"Good for them, but what does this have to do with me?" I teased. I understood perfectly well where the conversation was heading.

"Mr. Newman owns a movie theater in San Bernardino. He is looking for a bride from a similar background for his son."

"And? I am supposed to be that bride?" I laughed at the absurdity of Father's proposition. "This is not a laughing matter, Sophia. This man was serious."

"Okay," I replied. "I'm all ears."

"He is looking for a nice, Jewish girl from Czechoslovakia. He seems honest and straightforward, and is interested in meeting us," Father said.

"And how is this going to happen?"

"I have invited him over for dinner. You can see for yourself and then . . ." he didn't finish his sentence.

"So when is he coming?" I asked. "He will let us know within a month."
"Fine," I answered.

Even though it seemed funny at the time, I was intrigued by the possibility of going to Venezuela.

"This winter, he is coming for a vacation in the Tatra Mountains,"
Father said. "He will stop by for a visit."

"Do you know which hotel he'll be staying at?"

It just so happened that my friend Helga was working as a receptionist at a ski resort in the Tatra Mountains. I often visited her there on weekends. After Timka's marriage and subsequent move, Laura's departure, my sisters' marriages, and my failed escape attempt, Helga was the only friend I had left.

"I'm not sure," Father answered. "He'll be in touch upon his arrival."

All I could think was that Venezuela was closer to America than Czechoslovakia was. But I didn't let my father see my excitement. "I'm looking forward to meeting him," was all that I said. Father smiled lovingly, caressed my shoulder, and kept silent for the rest of our trip.

At the dirt road above the village, in front of the small overgrown forest, we came to a stop.

Since leaving Porubka at the age of six, I had returned only a few times, and I was curious to see what new developments had taken place. But unlike me, nothing had changed, and the little village looked just the same.

The Jewish cemetery was a jungle. The grounds were neglected and overgrown with weeds, bushes, and shrubs, and all of the gravestones had been abandoned or damaged. Wild grass grew up to my knees. Father seemed a bit uncomfortable, since as a *Kohen*, a descendant of the early priestly tribe of Israel, he was not allowed to enter a cemetery. According to ancient custom, *Kohens* are prohibited from coming in contact with dead bodies. In fact, when a *Kohen* dies, they are buried close to the walls of the cemetery, so that their descendants can draw as near as possible to their grave sites.

My father knew exactly where his father's grave was located in what little remained of the original cemetery. If not, it would have been impossible to find. The grounds were so overgrown with thorns and thistles that in order to prevent being scratched, we had to wrap our exposed skin in plastic bags. As we made our way through the brambles, we finally came upon the headstone. Father removed the overgrowth and revealed my grandfather's name spelled in Hebrew letters: Chaim Henry Manisevic.

As we stood in silence, I began to pray to my grandfather. I had never met him – he'd died in 1938 – but I felt connected to his spirit. All of a sudden, a swell of emotion overtook me and I burst into tears. Begging for forgiveness, I made a solemn promise to my grandfather that were I ever to be blessed with a son, he would carry on his name. Chaim Henry had passed away long before I was born, but I was sure that were he still alive, he would understand me. Right then and there, I begged him to help me get to America. Then I made another promise, this time to myself. I swore that one day, when I lived in America, I would return to Porubka and care for this lonely forgotten cemetery.

The High Holidays came and went, and I returned to my usual routine in Kosice. In this make- believe society, where everybody was considered equal, you were paid the same salary for the same job, whether or not you performed your duties. Employment was a State requirement, but we were prohibited from having more than one job. Hence, we turned to smuggling and the black market in order to supplement our incomes.

CHAPTER TEN

꙰

Saving Money for My Escape

Czechoslovakia, Ukraine, Bulgaria in the 1970s

I F I WANTED to save money for my next escape, I would have to be resourceful. Money equaled freedom, and I could barely make ends meet with my office job. So I continued with my sewing, buying less expensive, higher quality fabrics in Poland and Hungary, and smuggling them across the border. Together with Helga, I produced handmade jeans, and the orders rolled in.

"Next stop, Ukraine," I proclaimed one day, as I sewed a zipper on a pair of jeans. "Look at us," Helga said, beaming. "We've gone international!"

We were thrilled by our success and couldn't wait to expand to the Ukraine and beyond. "Since you work at the hotel, you should be the one making contacts and networking," I said.

"We need money and a lot of it."

"Good point," said Helga. "You are quite the entrepreneur."

"Do you know what I did last weekend? I went to the Ukraine to meet up with our old friends from the Pioneer Exchange Camp."

"I can't believe it, Sophia. I had completely forgotten all about them. Why didn't I think to keep their names and addresses?" Helga said.

"I was raised to believe there is a reason why certain people enter your life, and you never know when you may need their help. That's why I kept in touch with the Ukrainians for all these years," I told her. "And guess what?" I continued. "It was quite obvious that we could sell anything at any price to the Ukrainians."

The next week, we gathered together our new merchandise, as well as the clothing that we had ready to sell at the flea markets, and packed it all in a duffel bag.

"Will these sell over there?" Helga asked, pointing to our jeans.

To make them look more enticing, I had cut out the original labels from Father's American shirts, my own American dresses, blouses, skirts, pants, bras and underwear, and sewed them on the back pockets of our jeans. An American label tripled, sometimes even quadrupled, a garment's value.

"I love it!" Helga said proudly.

"You'd better believe it," I said, as I struggled to close my overstuffed bag.

With huge bags slung over our shoulders, we left the house and headed east to neighboring Ukraine. As Ukraine was considered safe territory, we assumed that we would not be followed by the secret police, but one could never be sure. Undercover secret agents had their own *modus operandi*, and were easily detectable. They were just like termites: if you saw one, you knew that there were thousands more, and no method of fumigation could rid us of them. Their presence infested every aspect of our lives.

That night we didn't sleep at all. Helga had come over earlier in the evening, and we stayed up until midnight sewing, altering, mending, and putting the finishing touches on our merchandise. The bus to Ukraine left from the main square at four a.m. the following morning. We stealthily made our way into the silent night.

Thanks to the connections I had made through my jeans business, I had already gotten my passport back. I would give a pair of jeans to any-one who had family members in green uniforms – the men and women who dealt with passports. It was a pleasure to make a pair of stylish pants for important clientele, as it gave them a sense of pride and superiority. But most importantly, it gave *me* what I needed to continue manifesting my dream. It was a well-known fact that there were those who ruled, and those who *were* ruled. Growing up, Mother and Father often repeated this adage: "Where there are sheep untended, you must become the shepherd."

It was of utmost importance not to conform to the masses. I went through the gray days in my gray building, looking out my window at the other gray buildings covered by a gray sky, which subtly illuminated the gray faces of the people. On the outside, I was still the good girl, but inside, my flame continued to burn. I had to make it to America. Many shared that same dream, but the difference between them and me was that I was unstoppable. No matter how many detours and obstacles were placed in my path, I would persevere.

With my passport back, I was once again able to travel, although there were limitations. I was only permitted to visit other Eastern Bloc countries: Russia, Romania, Bulgaria, Hungary, or Poland. They were considered friendly neighbors, and within this limited radius, I was allowed to move freely.

"Are you sure our Ukrainian business partners will be waiting for us at the bus stop in Uzgorod?" Helga asked nervously.

"Without a doubt. They are more reliable than a Swiss watch," I reassured her. "We deliver the merchandise, negotiate the price, and the rest is up to them."

"Do you mean they will give us cash right on the spot?" she asked.

"Not right away. When we return in about two weeks with new merchandise, they will pay us for this delivery. Understand how this works now?"

"Yeah, but, I will let you negotiate the price since you do a much better job." "Now we understand each other," I said, smiling.

I recalled my Hungarian adventure with my sister Hanka, when we smuggled several yards of polyester fabric used as garment lining. We would wrap ourselves like mummies beneath our street clothes and smuggle the fabric to a nearby Hungarian town. There we sold them for triple the price, as in those days polyester lining fabric was in great demand. Unwrapping ourselves from the bolts of fabric, we would drop from a size sixteen to a size six in a matter of minutes.

Because of limits imposed by the government, we were unable to exchange as much currency as we needed, so smuggling was our only option. With the money we made selling our garment lining material, we were able to replenish our supplies of other products – sunflower seed oil, toilet paper, or fabric for new dresses – which were all hard to come by in Kosice back then. Only a few quality fabrics were available, which meant that no matter how they were cut and sewn, everyone still ended up looking the same. It was not an uncommon sight to be standing in line at the grocery store, with all of the women wearing different versions of the same dress.

The minute we boarded the bus and took our seats, Helga and I fell fast asleep. By the time we woke up, we had reached the Ukrainian border crossing. In Uzgorod, Sergey and Alyosha, our Ukrainian contacts, were already waiting for us at the checkpoint. They hadn't changed all that much from how I remembered them from our Pioneer Exchange Camp days. They still had the same big ears we used to tease them about, and sometimes even pulled on.

Our new business connection was officially sealed over a cup of hot Turkish coffee in a nearby restaurant, where we dined on cold pierogies and stale bread. We handed over the goods and arranged to meet again at the same place, same time, in two weeks. I knew the risks involved, but I had absolute faith in my Ukrainian partners. Adorned with American labels, our jeans sold very well. I exchanged all the rubles I earned in the Ukraine for Czechoslovakian crowns, and over the next few months, I watched with glee as my bank account grew and grew.

The visit from Caracas was just around the corner. Mr. Newman's imminent arrival rekindled my hope that I would one day leave Czechoslovakia and make it to America. When he finally arrived, ready to size up his potential daughter-in-law, Mother prepared a meal as if it were a small wedding – all the while dreaming of the big one to come.

The meeting with Mr. Newman went well and he was optimistic that I would indeed become his daughter-in-law. Upon his return to Caracas, he sent me pictures of his son, his house, and the rest of his family. I fell madly in love with the picture of my future Venezuelan husband in my wallet, and would kiss it goodnight. Meanwhile, Mr. Newman would write letters by proxy for his son, as I studied Spanish with a passion, consuming every book I could. One day, I hoped, I would be able to communicate with my future Venezuelan husband, and for the next six months, we continued our correspondence.

The big day was drawing closer, and Mother could not stop herself from buying more and more linens for my dowry. She had already amassed so many Damascus linens from Tuzex, the only store in Kosice that sold Western luxury goods, that there was no room left to store them. It seemed as if the deal had been sealed, but then reality hit. In place of my future loving husband, a letter came from his father. The letter explained that his "adoring son" had fallen in love with a nice Jewish girl from Argentina. I was now out of the picture, and his picture was out of my wallet.

I couldn't stop crying. It seemed as though nothing was working out for me – not Switzerland, Venezuela or America. I ripped the picture of my once-future Venezuelan husband into tiny shreds and flushed it down the toilet. I felt like a fly, stuck in the glue of a trap, hopelessly flapping my wings, yet getting nowhere. It seemed that no matter where I looked, I couldn't see a way out. Regaining my senses, I realized that what I needed was a good vacation, so I called Helga to join me. I needed some time to recuperate and get out of this rut, where I found myself becoming increasingly irritated with everything and everyone around me.

On the sunny shores of Bulgaria's Black Sea, Helga and I lay out on the beach, absorbing every ray of sun in pursuit of the perfect tan. When the sun went down, we'd hit the disco, where we danced until the wee hours of the morning. We stayed in Bulgaria for only a week, as the tourist season was in full swing in the Tatra Mountains and Helga had to return to her job. Feeling happy and relaxed, we left the Golden Sands beach, a famous East European resort, and took the train from Sofia, Bulgaria to Budapest, where we would transfer to Kosice.

"That was great," Helga said, as she took her seat on the train. "Come to think of it, we really needed this." Her once-pale skin had turned a golden bronze.

"The world is a mystery," I said. "Some people are born lucky, and others spend their lifetimes searching for happiness."

"Not us," she said, smiling.

"Once we get back home, we might need another vacation just to recuperate from this one," I joked. "After all, we still have a lot of work ahead of us."

Everything went smoothly at the border crossing between Bulgaria and Hungary. We slept the whole way and woke up at the central train station in Budapest. Feeling recharged, we stepped into the warm Hungarian night and ran to catch the connecting train to Kosice. But as luck would have it, we had just missed it.

"What are we going to do now?" I asked, although I wasn't particularly worried. "The next train leaves at six in the morning," Helga said.

"We have some Hungarian money left over," I said. "It's not enough for a night in a hotel, but we can still afford a nice dinner. Let's at least enjoy ourselves."

We decided on our favorite restaurant, Matyas Pince, which was renowned for its fish soup.

After storing our luggage in train station lockers, we walked through the lit-up city until we reached the restaurant. Since Budapest was a mere four-hour train ride from Kosice, we both knew our way around the Hungarian capital.

At the restaurant, I ordered us two glasses of red wine and a plate of

Hungarian salami. At the next table, we noticed two young guys checking us out. They arrived at our table before the wine did, introducing themselves as Giancarlo and Piero, two charming Italians. Through a combination of broken Italian (learned from listening to my beloved Italian music), my high school Latin, and the remnants of my Spanish – not to mention hand signals – we were able to convey our predicament.

Nobody slept that night.

We danced the night away, hopping from bar to bar, until the early hours of the morning. It was a stellar night for everyone. We exchanged addresses at the train station, and our Italians acted as bodyguards until we heard the train whistle. Giancarlo wished me well with a gentle "*ciao bella,*" and as I found my seat, I could still feel the weight of his stare. When the train pulled out of the station, I thought how much better life was in Budapest. My heart sank. Vacation time was over.

From the savings I had been accumulating from my Ukrainian ventures, I was able to buy my own apartment. It was a small, co-op studio apartment in Kosice, not far from my sister Hanka. I was able to skip the years-long waiting list through the oldest trick in the book: bribery. I would stuff envelopes with cash and send expensive bottles of foreign liquor to anyone with connections. Soon enough, I was happily ensconced in my new home.

Owning your own home, especially for a young, single girl, was quite an accomplishment in those days. But what nobody knew was that my co-op was essentially another foil. By owning something as important as an apartment, I became less suspicious and seemed less apt to flee. From the outside, it seemed as if I was finally establishing my future right there in Kosice.

The most important thing in my apartment was my sewing machine, as I rarely left its side. Sergey and Alyosha were becoming more and more demanding, insisting that I travel to the Ukraine with new merchandise on a more regular basis. Once, in the dead of winter, when I made the journey alone, they treated me to lunch at a popular restaurant in the city. While we ate, none of us noticed that someone had stolen my beautiful red shearling coat, which Mother had just bought me for my birthday. As it was freezing cold, I opened the suitcase filled with my merchandise and pulled out a coat. But then I quickly put it back, worried that I was cutting into my own profits. I ended up wearing only a sweater.

When we reached the border on the way back home, I was ordered to get off the bus. My stolen fur coat had been officially declared on my customs form, and so once again, I had to go to war with the border police. I felt as if I were turning into my mother, fearing and despising anyone in uniform.

"So, Comrade Manisevicova, you are insisting that your fur coat was stolen in a restaurant?" the officer asked, during the grueling interrogation.

"Yes," I replied, looking him straight in the eyes. "Had you noticed anyone suspicious around you?" "No, I did not."

I watched as he jotted down my answers. "What is the value of that fur coat?"

"For me, it was priceless," I said. "It was a gift from my mother."

"Go to the waiting room until we write up the report. After that you may leave."

"This is unbelievable," I mumbled to the woman sitting next to me. "I get robbed and they treat me like I'm the criminal."

The woman was surrounded by more luggage than I'd ever seen. "Tell me about it," she said, and turned to her husband.

"Where are you heading?" I innocently asked. They looked at each other and shrugged. "Pardon me," I said. "I'm just curious,"

We sat in silence for a few minutes, before she turned to me, looked me straight in the eyes, and proudly announced, "We are moving to Israel."

"Did you say Israel?" I practically choked on my own words.

"We are Jews. We finally got permission to move there," the woman said. "I am also Jewish!" I exclaimed.

"I thought you were," she said, smiling. "I heard them say your name." The sense of communion overwhelmed us both.

"I don't want to seem nosy, but how were you able to get this far? Please, tell me, give me a hint. I would love to go there, too," I said.

"It has been a long and arduous journey," she answered. "The moment we submitted our applications, we instantly lost our jobs. We were told that since we wanted to leave so badly, Israel could take care of us. We were treated like traitors. People began pointing fingers at us and whispering behind our backs."

"I can totally relate," I said, confiding that I had once been turned back from the border in a botched escape attempt.

"It was an unpleasant process to get this far, but I can assure you that it's possible. I will provide you with a lead, but keep it to yourself. Go to

Rome, and once you are there, get in touch with the Hebrew Immigrant Aid Society, HIAS. They will help you," the woman said.

"Comrade Manisevicova, you can go now. Your report is done," the officer informed me. "Thank you," I said, and gave the unknown couple a glance of gratitude. I may not have my coat any longer, I thought, but I had received something far more valuable in return: information about Rome and HIAS that could help me realize my dream.

The man kept his eyes on the ground, but managed to give me an encouraging smile out of the corner of his mouth. I knew that he was wishing me well, and his smile filled me with hope and determination such as I'd never before felt. My faith had been restored, and I knew with certainty that I would escape my Communist prison soon enough. All roads led to Rome.

꒰

CHAPTER ELEVEN

A Second Chance to Escape

Czechoslovakia, Italy, 1979

SINCE THAT FATEFUL EVENING in Budapest when Helga and I missed our train, I had maintained correspondence with our new Italian friends, Giancarlo and Piero. Several months later, Giancarlo contacted me to say that he and Piero were planning a trip to the Tatra Mountains for New Year's Eve. They wanted to peek behind the Iron Curtain for themselves, they said, as all the stories we'd shared in Budapest had made it sound so exotic and surreal. It was then winter 1979, and I was 25 years old.

On New Year's, Helga and I happily met our Italian friends in the lobby of the Patria Hotel. We welcomed in 1979 with a bottle of fine Italian Champagne and danced all night to Italian pop music.

Dreaming of Rome, I had studied the Italian language and could practically see myself prancing around the Piazza Navona.

From the moment I saw Giancarlo, it was clear to me that he was interested in more than just a friendship. There had to be something more than the Slovakian mountains motivating him to drive through Europe in the dead of winter, I figured. Unfortunately, I wasn't ready for anything serious, and Giancarlo was clearly hurt. On the last day of the visit, I could feel his injured pride as he handed me a gift. It was a silver owl pendant, a good luck charm that his sister had bought for me in Greece.

"Grazie," I said, as I put away my new talisman.

Piero gave Helga a laughing clown pendant, and we all bid farewell, thinking it would be our last goodbye.

When spring came, I signed up with a travel agency for a two-week trip to Rimini, Italy. The tour would depart on June 1 from the city of Bratislava, which gave me several months to plan. More than five years had passed since my last escape attempt, and I was determined that this time I would succeed.

All the odds were in my favor: I had a brand new passport, a beautiful apartment, an excellent job, and a false romantic relationship that appeared serious. When I requested permission for vacation leave from my boss, I told her that I was visiting Italy for a final fling, since I'd soon be a married woman. Sporadic visits from Marian, with his usual bouquet of fresh flowers, created the impression that our relationship was moving to the next level.

The officers in charge of travel permits, however, came to a different conclusion, and they refused my application. My hands were shaking as I read how the men in green uniforms had reached their decision. According to them, I had missed the deadline. This was, of course, nonsense. The date on the stamp was a clear indication that it had been sent in time, even a few weeks early. Obviously, they applied different calendars to different people.

There was no time to waste. During my lunch break, I ran to the visa office to fight for my rights. The higher ranking officials took much longer lunch breaks than the rest of us, so I had to wait for what seemed like an eternity. I had skipped my own lunch to get in line, but there were already twelve people in front of me.

"Honor to work," I pronounced the appropriate Communist greeting as I approached the window. "It seems there must be some mistake with my application."

As the officer reviewed my documents, he realized that the application dates were, in fact, correct. Shaking his head, he said, "Comrade Manisevicova, although an error has been discovered, the department head's decision is final and non-negotiable." He was so embarrassed, he couldn't even look me in the eye.

"You can't be serious," I said. "I plan to appeal this decision." "Goodbye. Next!" he shouted from behind the window.

"Someone will pay for this!" I shouted, hiding my face so that no one would notice my despair.

"It's nothing but lies!"

Feeling desperate, I ran to Tuzex and bought the most expensive bottle of cognac I could find. With the bottle tucked under my arm, I returned to the passport and visa office building. First I went to the women's room to fix my makeup and calm down, and then I headed straight to the department chief's office, with the bottle of cognac protruding from my purse.

"Honor to work," I repeated the customary greeting.

"Do you have an appointment, Comrade?" the secretary asked, as I blithely entered the office. "Yes, he is expecting me," I replied.

The secretary saw the bottle poking out of my purse, and with a look of uncertainty, she let me enter. The department chief, a fat little man in a green uniform, sat behind his desk looking as if he owned the world. His chest was covered with shiny medals and his squinting brown eyes were barely visible in the folds of his hideous face.

"Honor to work, Comrade," he said, amazed by my sudden presence. "Manisevicova," I added. "Honor to work, comrade chief officer." "Your name, Comrade?" he coldly asked.

"Manisevicova," I repeated. "How can I help you?"

Realizing he was getting angrier by the second, I quickly handed him the bottle of cognac. "Excuse me, comrade chief officer, this is for you," I said. "I apologize for the inconvenience." He inspected the bottle, and with a well-rehearsed motion, placed it in one of his many cabinets. I could tell he was beginning to soften his stance.

"Sit down, Comrade," he said, and offered me a chair.

I felt as if the slits in place of his eyes were like an X-ray machine, boring through my very being, exposing all.

"You refused to process my travel permit to Italy, but I don't understand why. I followed protocol to the letter," I told him. "I am planning a two-week vacation before my wedding, which is just around the corner. I paid in full, it's not refundable, and I am due to depart in less than a week. I have a new apartment in Kosice, a great job, and have no intentions of not returning home," I said, all in one breath.

The department chief just sat there motionless, peering at me in silence.

"One moment, and I will look into your file," he said, as he heaved his bulk out of the chair and lumbered towards the metal file cabinets.

"Thank you. I greatly appreciate it."

I couldn't help but wonder whose destinies might be alphabetically stored in those files.

Returning with my file, he arranged his mass in the well-worn desk chair. Stains of sweat in the shape of the Soviet Union formed under his arms, and with that arrogant, smug smile, he appeared thoroughly unsympathetic. As I sat twitching and sweating on the other side of the desk, he flipped through page after page. "So I see you have an aunt in America, and also some family in Israel," he mumbled, almost inaudibly.

I could not contain myself a moment longer.

"I know why this is happening to me. It's because I am Jewish. You should be ashamed! This was supposed to be my last vacation before my wedding. Why do I have to suffer this mistreatment?" I continued with my tirade, growing more enraged with every word. "Five years ago you sent me back home from the border. Didn't my parents suffer enough? It's been over thirty years since the Holocaust, but I feel as if I'm in Auschwitz right here and now, just like my own mother once was. How am I supposed to feel proud of my country when I suffer this kind of abuse?"

He looked at me with an expression of pure shock.

"We are Communists, and that is what we believe in," he said, defending himself and his party.

I was not sure, however, whether he was trying to convince me, or himself, that we fully believed in Lenin, Moscow, and all the other ludicrous propaganda crammed down our throats. I pleaded with him to give me my travel permit. With a motion of his hand, he signaled that he would try to help. As his stubby fingers dialed a phone number, he said, "Give me a few minutes."

He called my boss, who was aware of my wedding plans. As I knew she would, she declared that I was one of her best workers, as well as a role model for others. Luckily for me, she also happened to be his friend. With an inconspicuous gesture of his hand, he alerted his secretary to issue my travel permit on the spot.

I was stunned that the impossible had happened. We cordially shook hands and he said, "Honor to work, comrade." Answering back, "Honor to work," I hoped it would be the last time in my life I had to utter those words. I walked out into the sunshine and took a deep breath. Suddenly, I wanted to kiss all those gray unknown faces I saw walking down Leninova Street.

Several days before my departure, I finally confided my plans to my sister Hanka. She was the only one I told. I also asked her to inform our parents, after I confirmed that I had landed in a safe place. I packed only one suitcase with what I needed. In order not to raise any suspicions, I left the rest of my belongings behind in my apartment. Finally, I handed my sister the keys, hugged her goodbye, and rushed off to bid my parents farewell.

Standing in the kitchen, I told them that I'd be visiting the Balaton Lake Region, a popular summer resort in Hungary. I was in and out quickly, as I didn't want them to suspect anything. There was always the possibility that the secret police were following me. As I held back tears, we hugged and kissed each other for what might be the last time. I loved my parents more than anyone in the world, and I was sure that they would not only forgive me, but one day would feel proud.

"See you later," I said, as I waved goodbye.

The first day of June came before I knew it. After an hour-long flight to Bratislava, I joined the other tour group members on Bajkalska Street. On the bus, I sat next to the window, halfway to the back of the bus, so I wouldn't have to talk to anyone. That's how nervous I felt. When we reached the Austrian border, I nearly had a panic attack. My palms felt clammy and my heart sped. The endless parade of uniformed officials stamping papers, inspecting buses and interrogating travelers unnerved me, to say the least.

Suddenly, we started to move again. I expected the bus to come to a halt at any moment. I imagined myself being led away in chains, escorted back to my prison cell by men in green uniforms. When we approached Schwechat Airport near Vienna, I began to breathe a bit easier. It was there that I stepped out onto West European soil for the first time.

Leaning against the bus, I lit a cigarette. As I inhaled the strong taste of Sparta tobacco, I noticed a billboard advertising Marlboro cigarettes. I was so accustomed to seeing billboards used only for propaganda that it took me aback. It was hard to imagine a slogan other than "With the Soviet Union Forever," or something similar, splashed across the cityscape. I would no longer be subjected to the daily onslaught of propaganda, I thought. Freedom was right at my fingertips.

My face was glued to the bus window the whole way to Rimini. As we drove, I took great notice of the people, the cars, and the gorgeous countryside. Everything seemed to look so different from how it looked on my side of the Iron Curtain.

When we arrived at the Hotel Astoria, a seaside resort, we were assigned rooms and given keys. I had to share a room with two middle-aged women, and I could swear that one or both of them worked for the Secret

State Police. Because we were one of the first tour groups to arrive, no one collected our passports to lock in the hotel safe until our departure.

I was the youngest in the group, and from day one, I had a great time. I went swimming, shopping, and ate gelato with handsome Italian guys I met on the beach. My pretend wedding quickly faded from memory. As the days flew by, my two roommates paid less and less attention to me, and the moment I'd been waiting for finally arrived.

From the local post office, just a short distance from our hotel, I called Giancarlo in Rome. I surprised him by announcing in fluent Italian that I was in Rimini. Would he like to come for a visit? I asked. Naturally, he jumped at the chance, and we made plans to meet at the post office in two days. I spent 48 excruciating hours waiting for the moment to arrive. When I made my final exit, the other tour group members were already having lunch in the downstairs restaurant. "Your soup is getting cold!" they said, as I passed by.

"Not today. I'm meeting a new friend I met at the beach," I told them, pretending to smile. "What is she up to? Isn't she about to get married," I could hear some of the gossipy women whisper to one another. Others just smiled and shrugged, unconcerned with whether or not I was having one last fling with a good-looking Italian guy.

Back in my room, I began to pack my bag but soon realized it was a bad idea. Carrying a large bag would only draw unwanted attention, so I unpacked nearly my entire suitcase. I took only one pair of underwear, a bikini, a small notebook with names and addresses, my passport, my wallet containing $60, and a vial of perfume, all stuffed in my small handbag. I had to leave all of my prized possessions behind, but the truth was that I had already left behind the most valuable thing of all: my family. I took out a piece of paper and wrote in bold, capital letters: DON'T LOOK FOR ME AND DON'T WAIT FOR ME! I placed it on my bed, between the pillow and the sheets. Finally, I stepped out into the warm, sunny, free new day.

As I made my way to the post office, my hands shook and my legs wobbled. I felt both thrilled and terrified at the same time. My handsome Giancarlo was already there, waiting for me in front of the post office, holding a bouquet of flowers in his hand. Leaning against his shiny Fiat Lancia, he flashed a big smile.

"*Bella mia*," he said, as he lifted me off my feet and kissed me.

"*Mi fa piacere*," I said, unable to stop laughing.

"Let me take you to lunch. Where would you like to go?" "Take me to Rome!" I replied.

"Where?" he asked, shaking his head in disbelief. "You heard me. And please, let's hurry."

As we sat down in the car, I informed him that he was about to become my partner in crime. I was defecting not just from my tour group, I told him, but also from Czechoslovakia. I explained how I planned to go to America with the help of HIAS, an organization in Rome that helped Jews emigrate.

As I watched Giancarlo's facial expression go from happy to shocked, I realized that he was proud of me on one hand, but he also felt used and disappointed, on the other. It was as if he played second fiddle to my dream.

"Giancarlo," I said. "This is the most important moment in my life thus far."

"Sophia, you know you mean the world to me, but I've never had an experience like this before, and I'm not certain what you expect of me."

"What I expect of you is to get me to HIAS in Rome as quickly as possible. I couldn't ask for a better friend to share this moment with. Remember the owl you gave me on New Year's Eve? Well, guess what? I wear it all the time for good luck," I said, as I pulled the silver pendant out from beneath my blouse.

"I'm in," Giancarlo said definitively. I didn't have to ask him twice.

As the road to Rome unfurled before me, I felt as though I were dreaming while fully awake. It all seemed so utterly surreal.

Giancarlo brought me to the home of his sister Ambretta, who lived with her husband, Enzo, and their 12-year-old daughter, Vanessa. In Ambretta's living room, I regaled them with tales of my life back home. By the time the last words had left my lips, I had inherited a new family. Crying and obviously moved, Ambretta promised to help and support me as if I were her own sister. I pointed at the owl pendant around my neck and said, "Look, you already are."

In her kitchen, we prepared an amazing dinner. For hours and hours, we ate, sang, and drank glass after glass of delicious Italian wine. Giancarlo's other sister, Loredana, joined us with her husband and a host of others friends, including Piero. Giancarlo could not take his eyes off of me for the entire meal.

"Bella, you are amazing," he said. "Look what you have done. They are all entranced by you." "If not for you, I wouldn't be here in the first place. Because of what you risked for me, I am indebted to you for life." I kissed him on his forehead and squeezed his hand. "You will always hold a special place in my heart," I said, smiling through my tears.

Ambretta and Enzo would not let me leave their house for the remaining days of my trip. They feared I'd be discovered by secret agents in trench coats, or the Communists, who could be combing the streets of Rome right now, searching for me as we spoke. The one place I was allowed to go to get some fresh air was the balcony. During those long hot days of summer, I would talk to Enzo's parakeets on the balcony, while Ambretta and her sister dressed me up in new clothes. Every day brought a new gift, and by the end of the first week, I had a complete summer wardrobe.

On June 14, 1979, I walked the streets of Rome a free woman. The tour group finally left Rimini, and I sprouted new wings. I fell in love with the city; with its coffee shops, piazzas, aromas, traffic, fashion, oleander, language, and of course, its food. I couldn't get enough. I was in Roman seventh heaven, built on the seven Palatine hills.

While I still glanced over my shoulder occasionally, my fear of being followed and deported was slowly diminishing. I never tired of the Roman statues, the magnificent architecture, the espresso, or the gelato served with whipped cream. I even loved the sound of all those horns honking and the stray cats screaming in the night – all part of "La Vita Italiana."

In a famous department store called Coin, near Piazza del Appio, Ambretta and I spent most of the day admiring the Italian fashions. How I adored the designs, styles, colors, and fabrics I saw in the windows. Everything looking so feminine, and most importantly, well-made. I couldn't resist trying on different outfits, running in and out of the fitting room like a kid in a candy shop. On my first day of real freedom, Ambretta bought me my first real designer dress. I was so touched that I promised myself to one day repay her the favor.

Rome and I, what a team we became. When I finally decided it was safe to call home, I went to the post office at Piazza San Silvestro to place the call. Father picked up, and through tears that smudged my makeup, I was able to convey the message that I was fine and did not plan to return. I begged Father not to worry about me, and ended our conversation by promising to keep him abreast of any new developments.

The next morning, Giancarlo drove me to the HIAS headquarters on

Via Santa Regina Margarita. As we drove through the crowded streets, I heard the voice of the Russian Jewish woman I'd met at the border crossing echoing in my head. "Go to Rome and find HIAS," I kept hearing. "They will help you."

At the HIAS headquarters, I was interviewed by the head of the emigration department. After a lengthy discussion, during which I described my experiences and current situation, along with my desire to go to America, she agreed to take my case. I was assigned a social worker, a Polish Jewish woman named Matylda Hason, who reassured me that it would not be long before I made it to America. For the first time, I truly felt that life was beautiful.

Together with my new-found family and friends, I visited as many different restaurants as I possibly could, trying new dishes and gulping down old favorites. Those Italians, always trying to outdo one another with their expressions of love and care for one another, including me. I was so pleased with the way things were going in Rome, I expected nothing but good news from HIAS. The following day, suntanned and wearing a light blue summer dress, I entered Matylda's office.

"Come in, Sophia," she said, giving me a warm welcome. "How do you like Rome?" "I adore this city," I answered.

"Well, that's good, because it looks like you will have to stay here longer than expected," she said.

My heart sank. "Why, what happened?"

"It has to do with your aunt, Blanca Swartz. That is her name, correct?" I nodded my head.

"When we contacted her for verification, she said she had no clue as to who you are, and that she knows no one by the name of Sophia Manisevicova."

"But that's impossible," I exclaimed, as I burst into tears.

"Either your aunt has denied you, or something else is going on," Matylda said, with an air of suspicion.

Over and over again I asked myself, "Why would she do this me?" She and my mother were the only members of the family to survive the Holocaust. This information made no sense. Handing me a tissue, Matylda tried in vain to calm me down. "Try to relax. I will speak with my boss," she assured me. "Go home and sleep on it, and come back tomorrow. We'll have more information for you then," Matylda said, as she walked me to the door.

"But you do believe me, don't you?" I asked, struggling to speak through my tears. "You know I'm telling the truth?"

"Yes, I do. I've come across many difficult cases while working here and I can assure you there is a reason for everything. Things always work themselves out for the best in the long run, so please stop worrying."

As I cried the night away, I couldn't stop thinking about the fact that my own family had denied me. The idea of it was unfathomable. Weeping and sniffling, I pleaded with God over and over again,

"Why me? Why is this happening?"

The next day, with puffy eyes and no makeup, I nervously returned to Matylda's office. "Sophia, you will get to America. I just need for you to be a bit more patient, as it might take a little longer than anticipated," she said. "And don't forget you love Rome, so why not make the best of the extra time you have to spend here? Besides, I have a proposition for you. Based on your file, and with your knowledge of Italian, Russian, Hungarian, Polish, Czech, and of course, Slovak, we think you could be quite useful in our office. You will still receive the financial support from HIAS, *and* earn some extra money. How does that sound to you?"

Her words were a soothing balm for my aching soul. "But what about getting to America?" I asked.

"You will get there, only instead of to Chicago, we might have to send you somewhere else, like Utah, for example," she told me.

"*Utah*?" I asked.

"Utah is still in America!" "But I want to go to Chicago."

"Let's see what we can do," she said, with a reassuring glance.

Gradually, I started to feel more at home living in Rome. Ambretta and I became very close, almost like sisters, and we spent much of our free time together. The family included me in their summer vacation to Terracina, a beautiful seaside resort just south of Rome. In their eyes, I was a heroine, not a refugee. I loved my new job assisting people who were in the same boat as I was, and in my free time I would window shop, indulging in the Italian fashion scene. I was amazed at the variety and quality of merchandise available in Rome compared with what we had back at Tuzex in Kosice.

I spent the Jewish holidays with Matylda and her family, even attending synagogue with them, and the summer flew by. While I was having the best summer of my life, the same could not be said for my family back in Kosice. After my successful defection, my parents and my sisters were interrogated by the secret police. First they came to my parents' home, then to my sisters,' then to Timka's, and then to the home of everyone that ever knew me. It was well understood that all mail was opened and read by the authorities before it even reached your house, if it ever did. So as not to jeopardize my family and friends any longer, I had to put an end to our correspondence, which made it even harder on all of us.

I tortured myself over what I had brought upon them and worried about the toll it was taking on my mother's health. I could only imagine how she must be worrying about me. Add to the mix the secret police, as well as the gossip – possibly the worst part of living in such a provincial city – and I could only imagine that my mother wasn't faring well.

It took the Slovak authorities some time to finalize my case, and I was among many others who were consequently sentenced as "dissidents due to illegal escape" from the Czechoslovakian Socialist Republic. Although I was now officially a criminal, after that sentence, the secret police refrained from bothering my family and friends again.

I loved Rome, but I still longed to get to America. Russian Jewish emigrants were departing for the United States on a daily basis, and yet here I was, still waiting my turn. I kept wondering why my Aunt Blanca had acted this way. What could be her reason? I wondered. "Everything will be as it should be; one day you will get it," my mother's words echoed in my ears, except this time, they came from Matylda's mouth. I had no choice but to persevere.

Toward the end of August, two new refugees from Kosice arrived at HIAS. My curiosity was insatiable, and I could not wait to find out who the lucky ones were. I ran down the stairs and was thrilled to see that they were, in fact, my friends. Richard had plans to go to his uncle in California, and the other one, Rudy, together with his wife and two young daughters, planned to settle in Brooklyn, where his sister resided. I helped to secure accommodations for them in nearby Ladispoli, a small town just outside of Rome, and reassured them that everything would be fine.

They received the same support from HIAS that I did and anxiously awaited their day of departure. We were all ready to jump at a moment's notice. The three of us waited for our interviews at the U.S. embassy in Rome, where we were told that the consul was supposed to grant us political asylum. The consulate was in dire need of an interpreter, so, based on my linguistic skills, I offered my services. HIAS wanted to speed up the process too, since expenses were rising now that Richard and Rudy, along with Rudy's family, were availing themselves of their services.

The embassy approved me as a nonprofessional interpreter. The American consul was provided with documentation of our experiences trying to escape the Communist regime, in addition to the religious reasons that had caused us to flee our homeland. We answered the questions they provided, and were subsequently granted political asylum in the United States of America.

The next day, Matylda welcomed me with the good news. "You are going to Chicago. We contacted your aunt, and she will be waiting for you at the airport," she said, with a slight hint of mystery in her voice.

"Thank you," was all I was able to say.

Matylda put her arm around me as if she had read my mind and explained that my aunt had not, in fact, denied me. "She knew that by doing this, it would enable you to secure funds from HIAS. As your sponsor, if she were to say yes at that time, she would have had to finance you out of her own pocket."

Now it all made sense. "Matylda, I can't thank you enough for everything you have done for me." We hugged tightly and bid farewell.

By October 24, I was on a flight to Chicago. Richard left the next day for San Francisco, and a week later, Rudy and his family were en route to New York. I said my goodbyes to Giancarlo, Ambretta, the entire family and all my friends, promising that I would stay in touch. I assured them that our extraordinary relationships would not end with my departure. On the contrary, I would never forget their hospitality, I said, and to this day, I can still hear their joyous shouts of "Americana!" at a goodbye dinner party that was held in my honor.

❧

CHAPTER TWELVE

Touchdown

America, 1979

O N THE FLIGHT TO CHICAGO, I lit one cigarette after another, trying to calm my buzzing nerves. I smoked Marlboro Lights, the American cigarettes I'd developed a taste for in Rome. I loved their cool, white filter and their smooth taste, which I preferred to the Spartas that everyone smoked in Czechoslovakia. I knew, of course, that smoking was bad for my health, but I also knew that one day, I would break free from the chains of addiction, just as I'd broken free from my Communist prison.

Between cigarettes and sipping weak overly-sweetened coffee, I did my best to distract myself from the fact that I was heading to an unknown land. As I fiddled with the cigarette nestled between my cracked lips, my heart thumped furiously. Here I was, leaving everything I knew behind. I had left my real home – Kosice – as well as my adopted, Italian home – Rome. My hands shook, chills ran up and down my spine, and my thoughts spun out in all directions. All the while, my aircraft was getting closer to the Land of the Free.

I was flying on Pan Am, which in those days, was considered the best American airline. The stewardess, a beautiful young woman with a heavy brown braid dangling over her shoulder, offered me a glass of 7-Up. As I switched from coffee to soda, I soon found myself staring at the other passengers, inspecting their faces for details.

My eyes landed on a beautiful dark-skinned Muslim woman, wrapped in a black embroidered veil. I focused on her only visible feature: her big dark eyes. Then my gaze turned to two young skinny Indian men in turbans, smelling of curry and wearing worn-out shoes with no socks. Finally, my eyes landed on a pair of noisy Americans, speaking so loud that I couldn't tell if they were vociferously agreeing with one another or arguing opposing points. Was this what it would be like in America? I wondered. Were all of them this loud?

A maelstrom of questions swirled through my head, but I didn't have a single answer. Would America offer me what I was so desperately searching for? Would it be the place I'd seen in my dreams? And would anyone even understand me? Not knowing what to expect, I began to feel as if I was running out of energy. I missed having a shoulder to lean on, a pair of eyes to gaze into, or another hand to hold in mine. I craved companionship; someone to reassure me that everything would be all right, and that I would be happy and successful in all my endeavors.

When we landed at JFK airport, and I saw the lights of New York City sparkling for the very first time, my heart nearly skipped a beat. After eight hours of travel, I should have been exhausted, but my excitement overrode any feeling of fatigue, and my body felt as if it were running on autopilot. I roamed about the airport, feeling that old familiar fear that something ominous was about to happen.

Too nervous to go through immigration, I let the two Indian men and the Muslim woman jump ahead of me in line. Standing back, I studied the faces of the immigration officers, trying to decide which one would be nice, not cause me any problems, or ask too many questions. At last, it was my turn, and I nervously stepped up to the booth.

"Hello," said a young officer, who seemed kind enough, despite the fact that he didn't smile. "Hello," I said back.

"How are you?"

As he inspected my passport, I kept my eyes wide open and my mouth shut tight. Then he looked me in the eye, and said, "Welcome to the United States of America." That was all there was to it. He issued my resident alien card right there on the spot. In a split second, I had become a legal resident of the United States.

From Kennedy Airport, I was shuttled with about twenty others to LaGuardia Airport, where I boarded my connecting flight to Chicago. The connecting flight was on Delta Airlines, and because of that, to this day, I am a loyal and dedicated Delta customer. With my new documents in hand, I waited impatiently for my beat-up, old suitcase to come off the conveyor belt. When it finally arrived, I found my aunt and uncle waiting for me in the arrivals area.

"You finally made it, my dear," my aunt said, as she hugged, kissed and squeezed the life out of me. She had the same posture and facial expressions as my mother, so I felt right at home.

"I am so happy to finally be here," I told Aunt Blanca. "Thank you so much for your help." I had 101 questions I was dying to ask her. "Aunt Blanca," I said.

"Yes, Sophia?"

"Despite the fact that you have never heard of me, here I am." "My dear, I hope they explained everything to you."

"They told me very little. I want to hear it directly from you," I said, as our eyes met.

"If I were to confirm that you were my niece, HIAS would never have helped you. This way you could rely on the agency that took care of the Jewish emigrants. I was told they would give you financial assistance, send you to school, or find you a job and take care of you until you were able to be self-sufficient," she said.

"Now I get it," I said, breathing a sigh of relief. I had not been abandoned, after all.

"I would never ever deny you. When they called me from HIAS, I immediately inquired as to what would be best for you. I also asked advice from my friends at the synagogue who had been through the same experience before I came to this heart-wrenching decision."

At that moment I felt so very proud of my Aunt Blanca. My eyes filled with tears and I gave her a big long hug. Now I understood what Matylda had meant when she told me, back in Rome that everything would be explained. As it turned out, my aunt had actually done everything possible to help me, and I am forever grateful. From that experience, I learned that things are not always as they appear on the surface, and to never jump to conclusions. Just as I learned in sewing, always measure twice before you cut once. I thanked my aunt over and over.

"Don't thank me. You should be proud of yourself. This was not a coincidence or sheer luck.

This was all you," she said proudly, and hugged me again. I humbly agreed.

"Being stubborn is sometimes a virtue, and even though your mother often complained about you, I always reminded her that if she left you alone, you would eventually choose the right path.

Welcome to America, my dear," my aunt gushed, in her mix of Czech, Slovak and English.

Julius and Blanca Swartz lived in a beautiful house in Evanston, Illinois, a heavily Jewish suburb of Chicago. The house was on a tree-lined street, and while it felt peaceful and calm, the city was a mere twenty minutes away. I still remember how, stepping in the door for the first time, I could smell the aroma of warm chicken soup simmering on the stove top. I followed my nose to the kitchen and found a pot filled to the brim with vegetables – practically an entire garden – with swirls of fat bubbling on the surface. As I remembered my own mother's chicken soup, a wave of nostalgia swept over me. It smelled exactly the same. This was not just chicken soup, I realized, but Jewish penicillin: the best medicine for body and soul.

Those first two days at Aunt Blanca's, I felt anxious and on edge. Thankfully, by day three, I was finally able to relax a bit. The smell of fresh linen filled the house, and I took comfort in my aunt's presence. After all, she so resembled my mother. None of the honking cars, or the constant hum of the television bothered me. I was simply happy to be there.

That first week, I did manage to call home. I told my parents that I had arrived safely and in one piece, and said how much I missed them. Later, I called Giancarlo in Rome to let him know I'd made it. But while I was overjoyed to be in America, the truth was that I had landed in a foreign city, and at times, I missed the familiarity of Rome. Here everything looked huge: the cars, airplanes, six-lane highways, skyscrapers all seemed like they had been built for giants. Even the billboards were five times the size of what I'd dreamed.

I knew there were no guarantees that she who wins the battle will win the war, and so I had my moments of doubt. At times, my chest would become heavy, my head would pound, and I would hear nagging whispers of insecurity with every decision I made. Suddenly, the past didn't seem so bad after all. I began to miss the V-club, the Basta Club, my illicit Ukrainian adventures, HIAS headquarters, and those endless dinners in Rome.

Here in Chicago, I had to start from scratch. I needed new friends, a job, a warm winter coat, money, and most of all, the ability to communicate in English. At that time, the only phrases I had mastered were the title of the Beatles song, "All You Need Is Love," and the slogan "Nobody can do it like McDonald's can," which I'd seen on one of those super-sized billboards. With such a limited vocabulary, how could I conquer the world? The first phrase sounded like a cliché, and the second one, no pun intended, was in really bad taste.

Shortly after my arrival, Aunt Blanca took me to visit the Jewish Social Service agency in Chicago. Until then, I had believed that being Jewish was somehow a disadvantage. This is what I had been told from a young age, and thinking it was simply the way of the world, I eventually got used to it. But suddenly, here at the Jewish agency, everyone was so cordial and helpful that my outlook changed in an instant. For the first time in my life, I began to feel that being Jewish might actually be an advantage. I was given phone numbers that I could call 24 hours a day, in case I needed help – with anything. I was also given financial assistance, and I made a promise to myself that when I was able to, I would pay them back in full.

Not long afterward, I got in touch with the American branch of HIAS and registered my new address. In return, I received a bill for the airfare and all of the other expenses I had accrued. It's simple mathematics: everything comes with a price. HIAS's mission was to give me all the financial, legal, and emotional support that I needed, but it was understood that once I got back on my feet, I would repay them. My mission was not only to pay back my debt, but to contribute a little more, in order to help other refugees on their journey to freedom.

Determined to overcome the language barrier in the shortest time possible, I enrolled in English classes at the local Jewish Community Center. Unfortunately, I never completed the course, not due to lack of effort, but due to the fact that I was surrounded by Russian Jewish immigrants. While I found my Russian skills improving, my English skills were not. I also didn't want to join the Russian clique, adopt their slang, or drink their cheap vodka, so I left the class as fast as I had joined.

It seemed to me that finding a job would be the best way for me to improve my English.

Through the employment agency, I was sent to work at a store in Evanston called Vogue Fabrics. The store was owned by two Jewish brothers, and we sold everything related to the world of fashion. From sewing machines to fabrics to buttons, patterns, and notions, we carried everything down to the smallest needle.

I was in heaven. Not only did I understand the materials and merchandise, but also the people. This was, after all, my expertise, and so I knew exactly how to advise our customers. I was passionate about fabrics, and I enjoyed caressing the beautiful silks, cashmeres and cottons that came from as far away as India. I stayed away from the synthetic fabrics, as they made me sneeze. I only liked real materials and real people.

The two middle-aged owners seemed to like me. Every day they would show up at work at the same time, looking groomed and dapper in dress shirts and perfectly matching ties. They embodied the quality of their business. Each morning, without fail, they took the time to stop by and ask, almost in unison, how was I doing. This scenario played out every single day, without fail. One day, after asking myself if they really cared about me, I decided to test them. I dressed up in a fancy dress and put on bright lipstick before I went to work in the morning.

As usual, my bosses saw me and asked, "How are you this morning?"
"I'm about to kill myself," I replied politely.

"That's nice," they said, and moved on.

As it turned out, I was not their favorite employee. They really didn't care how I felt each morning, or what my response was. My well-being was not of the utmost importance to them; they only cared that the store interior and rolls of fabric looked "nice." I was not just learning the language, but also figuring out the meaning behind certain overused American phrases. Every day, I got the message louder and clearer that not every question warranted an answer. Everything had its limits, especially in matters of business.

Gradually I became more independent and was finally able to stand on my own two feet. I left Aunt Blanca's house and moved into a studio apartment on Lunt Street, in the heart of Chicago. The move represented the first step in my process of reinvention. It was time to set down roots. Friends donated furniture and I decorated the apartment with a few simple things. Remembering my mother's words that one should always have something to eat, I filled my small refrigerator with kosher groceries.

Overall, I was doing fine. But I still had the nagging feeling that something in my life was missing. My job was satisfying, my English was improving, and I had a wonderful relationship with my aunt and uncle, but I did not leave my family and everything I knew behind to become the best salesperson at Vogue Fabrics. I said as much to Aunt Blanca, who came to visit me at work one day.

As we spoke, she kept urging me to go back to the customers, claiming, "No one pays you for talking to me."

"They don't have to," I replied.

One afternoon, I was sitting in my studio, sewing a button on a shirt, when the phone rang. I couldn't believe whose voice I heard on the other end – my old friend Laura! She had heard from her brother Marian, my make-believe fiancé, that I'd finally made it to America.

"Where are you? How are you?" I exclaimed, when I heard her voice. It had been nearly two years since we'd last seen each other.

"I'm still in Brooklyn, but no longer with the family my father sent me to. It was not easy in the beginning, but I'm fine now, and my father is happy that his escape plan worked out for the best," she said.

"Talk to me. Tell me everything."

"It was very difficult in the beginning and I was brokenhearted. So many nights I lay awake in my bed, living with relatives in Brooklyn, crying my eyes out. I didn't like it here in Borough Park, and all I wished for was to get on the first flight back home."

"But you stayed, didn't you?"

"Yes, I did. I was angry at my father and the whole world, and I did not understand my new family. They tried so hard to help me adapt to their ways, but they lived a completely different life than I was used to. It took some time, but now I love it here. Sophia, you must come to New York. You haven't seen or experienced anything like this city," she insisted.

"When will that be?" I asked, joyful at the prospect of seeing my dear friend once again. "Very soon," Laura announced.

"Are you coming to Chicago?"

"No, you will be coming to Brooklyn for my wedding," she said.

I almost dropped the receiver. I was so immersed in hearing her story that I forgot to tell her my own.

"This is why I'm calling you, Sophia. It's incredible how fate can shape our lives. After being here awhile, things improved, and I actually did fall in love again. If only you could have seen me before, waking up every morning with bloodshot eyes."

"I can only imagine," I replied. "Where will the wedding be held?" "Here in Brooklyn, of course. Will you be able to make it?" she asked. "Of course. I wouldn't miss it for the world," I happily answered.

Laura sounded so grown-up, so mature, and I could sense the contentment in her voice. She had already moved to the next level, while I was still waiting for my elevator, pushing those darn buttons. I was so happy for her, her future husband, and her entire family. But at the same time as I wished them well, I also envied their good fortune. I too wanted to fall in love and get married.

CHAPTER THIRTEEN

⅍

Moving to New York City

M Y BOSSES INVITED ME to join them for their seder, which was held on the first night of Passover. It evoked sweet memories of Passovers gone by at my family's home in Porubka, and later in Kosice. As far back as I can remember, my sisters and I would look forward to the Passover holiday with great anticipation. When reading from his pictorial Haggadah, Father would alter his voice, performing the part of each character until our jaws dropped, and we hung on his every word. I can still remember helping Father carry all of our special Passover dishes up the stairs, from the cellar of our building. I also remember my mother rushing around the kitchen, lovingly preparing cakes and other goodies from matzo meal. Her perfectly soft matzo balls would float like buoys in the steaming bowls of chicken soup. Perhaps most unforgettable, though, was her walnut cake with chocolate frosting, dipped in wine sauce for dessert.

My boss's son, who wore a ponytail and also worked at the store, was kind enough to pick me up and drive me to their luxurious home in a posh suburb of Chicago. The five tables set up in the basement were elegantly arranged. In the center of each table sat a plate with three covered pieces of matzo. The Seder plate was arranged according to tradition, bottles of wine were placed on the tables, and a leather-bound Haggadah was placed next to each Kiddush cup. A separate glass of wine for the prophet Elijah was set on one of the tables, signifying his welcome, as well as the Messianic meaning of this holiday.

To my great surprise, the kosher meal was catered rather than home-made. I looked around stunned, hesitated for a moment, and then I asked my boss's son, "Is this all kosher for Passover?"

100

"Of course it is," he answered, while I tried to formulate the next question in my head.

"All these fancy cakes and colorful pastries are really kosher? I've never seen anything like this made from matzo meal," I said.

"Yes, everything here is kosher. My parents order it from a famous bakery not far from here every year."

"I'm not used to being catered to," I said.

"I am sure there are more things that you are not used to," he said. "What?" I thought he was teasing me.

"The wine!" he said loudly. "What?" I asked again.

"We have to drink four full glasses."

"I know," I said, shaking my head in disbelief.

I couldn't stand those American know-it-alls. Of course I knew the order of the four cups of wine at the seder; it was one of the few traditions that women were required to participate in. I also knew how each of the four cups related to a different proclamation from the Exodus story, when the Jews were led out of Egypt.

"I will take you out." "I will liberate you." "I will save you."
"I will accept you as my people."

Well into my second glass of wine, at the time of "liberation," I could already feel a buzz coming on. By the time we were "saved," I felt my inhibitions slowly melting away, and everything started to appear even more grandiose and appealing, including the big loopy smile of my long-haired friend. I knew that I could not afford any social mishaps – he was my boss's son, after all – and on top of that, I was getting ready to leave for New York to attend Laura's wedding.

I reminded myself that he wasn't my type – since when did I like guys with ponytails? –and decided it must be all that wine. Was I turning into my mother? I wondered. Just as she had prepared my dowry for my Venezuelan husband before I'd even met him, here I was, picturing myself under the *chuppa*, the wedding canopy, with my boss's son, before we'd even kissed. Never mind that when I was sober, I wasn't even attracted to him in the slightest. At that moment, I regained my sanity and decided to call a cab. I quietly bade farewell to the Seder table, thanked my hosts, and returned to my studio apartment on Lunt Street.

After landing in New York City for Laura's wedding a month later, I remembered the "Midnight Cowboy," and how I'd imagined myself standing right there beside him, en route to freedom. Only the New York

City I found was very different from the one I'd envisioned. As Laura had described on the telephone, she lived in Brooklyn, not Manhattan, and her neighbors were not the sophisticated urbanites I'd imagined. Instead they were religious Jews. In Williamsburg, where she worked, they were members of the Satmar Hasidic community, an Orthodox Jewish sect that mostly hailed from Romania and Hungary. They were far more religious than anyone I had known growing up. I'd never encountered a Satmar, as almost all of them who survived had fled Eastern Europe following the Nazi genocide.

Laura's new husband managed a pharmacy in Williamsburg, where she worked filling prescriptions. Shortly after my arrival, the newlyweds tried to convince me to move to New York by asking me to work with them. They didn't have to do much convincing, as living and working that close to one of my oldest friends from Kosice was more than enough incentive to leave Chicago.

Standing behind that pharmacy counter with Laura was a welcome *déjà vu*. I was also able to sublet her old studio apartment in the Midwood section of Brooklyn, which made the transition even smoother.

Back in the Windy City, I quit my job, said my goodbyes to family and friends, and gave away all of my furniture, just the same way I'd gotten it. I sublet my apartment to one of the Russian girls I knew from English class, and packed the rest of my belongings into two suitcases. Once again, Laura and I were working together, side by side, in the pharmacy. The only difference was that it wasn't Kosice, but rather Williamsburg, the heart of Orthodox Jewish Brooklyn.

Needless to say, I experienced some serious culture shock. Here I was, all alone again, left to my own devices in an unfamiliar world. I missed my family and the ground I used to walk on. Even the clouds in the blue sky somehow felt different. I was seemingly free, amid my own people, and yet I still felt estranged from the masses, as if I didn't belong. The Satmar philosophy was alien to me. Walking down the streets of Williamsburg, I'd pass so many pregnant mothers, pushing their strollers with herds of children flocking around their legs.

It was also quite strange to see a mother and daughter pregnant at the same time, but because of their strict rules when it came to intimacy, it was not an uncommon sight. The men wore black suits and long black coats and had long curly sideburns called *peyes*, which they sometimes tucked inside their black or fur hats. The women wore long skirts, long-sleeved blouses, and regardless of the weather, they always covered their legs. Strict rules about modesty also meant that when a woman got married, she had to cut off most of her hair. From then on, she would wear a wig in public, so as not to attract unwanted attention from members of the opposite sex.

Out of respect for my new community, and as a way of fitting in, I began to wear those same long skirts and long-sleeved blouses that reached up to my chin. Meanwhile, my English stagnated, as I spent my days with Laura, speaking Slovakian. With a mostly Hungarian-speaking clientele at the pharmacy, even my Hungarian improved faster than my English.

I was eager to better understand the Satmar customs, which included men not being allowed to engage in small talk, make eye contact with, or take change from a woman. I was under the impression that all Hasidim followed their laws and customs to the letter, until one day reality hit. As a Satmar man handed me his prescription, he began engaging in small talk and even asked my name. As far as I knew, this was strictly forbidden.

Taken aback, I politely answered, "Sarah Rachel," in Hebrew.

Then my mind went blank. My heart began to race, and seemingly out of nowhere, I began to picture myself standing under the *chuppa* with this perfect stranger. It actually made sense, since marriage was the only thing on my mind those days. What if he's the one? I thought. Forget about fashion and the material world, I would cut my hair short and wear only long skirts from that moment forward. I'd also have to wear ugly shoes, but I wouldn't have to see them, since my pregnant belly would block the view until I was about fifty years old. Don't ask me what I was thinking.

I fantasized about changing him, making him more to my liking. We would fall in love with each other and elope. Maybe it was the ticking of my biological clock, or perhaps I just wanted to prove to myself and the world that I was worthy of love. With all of these thoughts swirling through my head, I looked down at his prescription. His name was Moishe. In my mind's eye, I was slowly cutting off Moishe's shiny *peyes* and shaving his thick black beard. Next I trimmed his hair and dressed him up in a crisp white shirt, sneakers, and a nice pair of blue jeans. Right there, in the midst of my vivid imaginings, stood a copy of Marcello Mastroianni; a tall slim man with dark eyes that pierced my heart – and all I was doing was nodding "yes." Moishe stood patiently, waiting for his medication. "In English, my name is Sophia," I said.

As my thoughts continued to multiply, he looked straight into my eyes and replied, "That is a beautiful name."

Then he looked away and fell silent.

I had clearly misinterpreted the whole incident. He was merely complimenting me on my name, not asking for my hand in marriage. At that moment, my Moishe Mastroianni liberated me from any notion that I had to conform to rules that I didn't understand, and nor wanted to follow. I placed his change on the counter in front of him, since he was not allowed to take it directly from my hand. His long black coat and black hat were obvious indicators of where he belonged. It became clear to me that
I did not.

I felt like myself again, at last. I would no longer pretend to be one of them, wearing their dark skirts and ill-fitting blouses. I am who I am, I decided. I had to accept myself as a child of God, one who would neither be judged, denounced, nor loved any less for being me. I no longer felt the need to pretend. Yes, we were all Jews, but we were all so very different.

I showed Moishe to the door, feeling grateful for our exchange. Now I knew I didn't have to prove myself to anyone. I wanted real love, not an arranged marriage. I wanted children, but not an entire soccer team. I wanted to show my wavy hair, not shave it. I wanted to be free to make my own choices. I wanted an equal partner in matrimony.

The next day, I walked into the pharmacy wearing my new tight-fitting Jordache jeans, and a v- neck tee shirt. It was a scorching hot day, and although my outfit turned some heads, nobody said a word.

Every woman I knew was trying to find me a match. These introductions sometimes soothed and flattered my slightly damaged ego, but aside from that, they always felt forced. Meeting a Satmar guy, I never got butterflies in my stomach or felt pangs of excitement stirring in my chest; I was running on fumes. According to the Satmar women, I had passed my prime and had clearly come to America looking for a suitable Jewish husband. They tried everything in their power to make it happen, introducing me to every available man they knew: friends, brothers, relatives, acquaintances, strangers – it didn't matter.

Whenever I overheard, "My brother has a friend who came to visit. He is our relative from the maternal side . . ." I knew that it would inevitably end up with the question of whether or not I was interested. What had I gotten myself into? I wondered.

One of my co-workers, a young pharmacist, told me he had a classmate and good friend from his years at the yeshiva whom he wanted me to meet. He raved about him, and insisted that we should at least have a conversation. I was open to the possibility, since as an unintended consequence of wearing tight jeans to work, I had been officially knocked out of the Orthodox running. This meant that my options were rapidly diminishing, and I was more than happy for the set-up.

My blind date, Sofio, was from an observant family that originally came from Tripoli, Libya. He was well aware that life existed beyond the walls of the yeshiva, and in addition, he spoke perfect Italian. Was this a coincidence? I wondered. How many Jewish Sofios could there be out there?

Whether I wanted to admit it or not, my biological clock *was* ticking in my ears, my chest, my veins, and throughout my entire body. I visualized every man I met as a potential husband, whether strolling the streets, sitting on the subway, or standing on line at the supermarket.

One afternoon, I wandered aimlessly and came across a movie theater where John Travolta's new movie *Urban Cowboy* was playing. By then, I was able to understand most of the dialogue, and when I heard the song, "Looking for Love in all the Wrong Places," I knew that now I was in the right place. Would Sofio be the one? I wondered. Was I finally looking in the right place at the right time?

We met that same evening. I immediately felt shivers run up and down my spine. This time it wasn't from the fear of police or an unplanned setback, but from a pure and genuine excitement at meeting Sofio, or Shushan, in Hebrew. He had a mysterious Bohemian quality about him and an unshaven olive-skinned face. After a pleasant dinner, we took a walk on the beach and spoke in Italian for hours. We philosophized about life and all its mysteries, and the unpredictability of fate. He was well-educated, analyzing words and their meanings. He loved art, as well as the more mundane down- to-earth things life had to offer. We also shared a love of Italian music.

The attraction was so strong that it made me think of that magnet my sister Hanka had described in her diary. With Sofio, I was living my dream of an American summer romance. I loved everything about him, including his creatively messy apartment, filled with books, cassettes, and photographs that were scattered all over the floor. Sofio was a talented photographer, and he hoped that his works would one day be shown in one of New York's top galleries – including the black-and-white portraits he took of me.

It was all the romance I could dream of, but I wanted something more.

I wanted to get married, to find a husband, to be where my mother wanted me to be: under the *chuppa*, ready to start a family. Each time I brought up the subject of marriage, Sofio would rebuff me, saying we had plenty of time. "Let's just have a good time and get to know each other better," he'd say. "As long as we love each other, there should be no pressure."

All signs pointed to the fact that Sofio had a fear of commitment. While his camera lens was clicking, I felt I was running out of time. So we broke up. Or did we? The chemistry between us meant we couldn't stay away from each other for long. The relationship had an on and off switch. At times, the lights shone upon us with all the brilliance of a carefree romance. At other times, it was a total blackout and the breach between us widened.

Sofio was no longer an option. I had looked in the wrong place.

Once again, my ego was bruised and I was hurting. If I couldn't make it in New York with Sofio, I decided, I'd make it on my own. I went back to the drawing board and enrolled in the Mayer School of Fashion Design on the corner of 37th Street and Sixth Avenue in Manhattan's Garment District. I left the pharmacy on short notice, and in order to make some extra cash, I sewed shoulder pads into jackets after school. On weekends, I apprenticed with a well-known designer named Terry Sherman, who owned Fine and Fancy, a boutique on Coney Island Avenue in Brooklyn.

At Fine and Fancy, we made custom-designed gowns and dresses for all occasions, including weddings, and bar and bat mitzvahs. Terry and I worked well together, and soon enough, she made me her personal assistant, as well as her co-designer. I bought my own sewing machine and she supplied me with the customers' orders.

As fate would have it, sewing brought me not only joy, money, and satisfaction, but also the much-desired love I was seeking.

❧

CHAPTER FOURTEEN

Meeting Mr. Right

New York City, 1980

GOING TO SCHOOL turned out to be a great decision. It gave me entrée into the world of high fashion, a world full of beautiful models – some thin, others outright anorexic – big-name department stores, bigger-name designers, and showrooms where I dreamed of one day selling my designs. The fashion industry was competitive, and if you weren't willing to put in what felt like hundreds of hours a week, you'd never make it. I considered my studio apartment, which was strewn with fabrics, to be my home office. Terry was an excellent mentor, not to mention one of my few English-speaking friends, and through hard work and talent, I did well in school.

Just a block away from the Mayer School of Fashion Design, on the corner of 36th Street and Broadway, was a kosher pizzeria called Jerusalem II. Their thin crust pizza was simply delicious, and the guy behind the counter was a real sweetheart. On the first day that my classmates and I went to Jerusalem II for lunch, he approached me just as we were leaving.

"How did you like it?" he asked, with a big smile. "Very much," I answered shyly.

"My name is Harry Fisher," he said, as he extended his hand. "Sophia."

"How are you doing, Sophia?" he asked, sounding even sweeter. "Great, and you?"

"Curious. I love your accent. It's so charming. Where are you from?" I'd heard this often.

"I'm from Czechoslovakia," I muttered, trying to catch up to my friends.

As I walked back out onto Broadway, blending in among the bustling crowds and yellow taxi cabs, I forgot all about Harry.

Because the pizza was so good, and the restaurant was so close, my friends and I returned. As I walked through the door and saw the smiling face of the guy behind the counter, I realized I'd forgotten his name. Just as it was the first time, the food was good, and the conversation even better. We devoured our slices until nothing remained on the flimsy white paper plates except for the oil that dripped all over them.

"Hey ladies, it's good to see you here again," Harry said as he joined our table uninvited. "We love it here. It looks like we are becoming regulars," I said, with a coy smile.

"I'm honored," he said, giving me a courteous bow.

"You know what they say, location is everything. Having great food and service doesn't hurt, either," I said.

"Would you allow me the pleasure of giving you a behind-the-scenes tour? Come with me, Sophia from Czechoslovakia, and I will show you around the kitchen."

"Why not?" I answered, and got up from the table. I could hear my girlfriends giggling as I left with my tour guide.

As we walked to the back, he pointed to the prep kitchen, the stoves, and then at a door. "That's my office," he said proudly.

"Your office?" I asked, a bit puzzled.

"Yes, I co-own this place with my brother," he answered. "We are being supervised by a *mashgiach*, a rabbi who oversees our kitchen and makes sure that the food is properly prepared according to kosher law."

"Oh, so that's how it works," I said, with a touch of amazement.

How would I know? Where would you find a pizzeria, let alone a kosher one supervised by a rabbi, in eastern Czechoslovakia? He wasn't trying to impress me, even though he did.

"I never thought I would end up in a business like this. I graduated from John Jay University with a degree in Forensic Science, but because of affirmative action, I couldn't find a job in my field. So I decided to join my younger brother Teddy and here I am."

"I can relate," I said. "Even though I had excellent exam scores, I was denied entry to the University of Prague because of quotas," I said.

"What did you plan to study there?" he asked. "Public Health."

"So how did you end up studying fashion design? That's about as far from Public Health as forensics is from pizza."

"I've always loved fashion, and I guess it was meant to be this way. I want to do what I enjoy,"
I said.

"Are you familiar with the city?" he asked, as he continued to show me around.

"Not really, since I live in Brooklyn. But I'm getting around much easier now that I've been here for a little while."

On the way back from the kitchen, he asked for my phone number. "You don't waste any time," I said.

"There is no time to waste," he said, laughing.

As I nodded in agreement, I noticed a photograph of a beautiful young woman sitting on his desk. Here we go, I thought. His wife's photo is displayed for all to see, and he wants my phone number? All men are the same. If only they would stop thinking with their testosterone.

"I'm sorry, but I don't think so," I told him.

"Okay, maybe not right now, but one day I hope you will give it to me," he said with an air of self-confidence.

"Whatever," I said, and laughed.

After my brief tour of the pizzeria, I rejoined my classmates at the table. On our way out, we linked arms and yelled, "We'll be back!"

"I hope sooner rather than later," the counter guy said. "See you later," I said.

"See you sooner," he shot back, smiling.

A few days later, I went back to the pizzeria by myself. Harry's face lit up the moment I walked in the door. I acted as if nothing had happened, but I did notice that big smile. I liked him too, but I knew to stay away from married men. It only meant inviting unnecessary problems and grief, which were not what I was looking for.

"It's good to see you again," he said.

"Hi, Harry." I called him by his name for the first time.

"Sophia from Czechoslovakia, what are you doing this Sunday?" "Nothing special. Why?"

"I would like to invite you for a Simchat Torah celebration," he said.

Simchat Torah, which comes at the end of Sukkot, symbolizes the completion of the Torah reading cycle. It's a joyful holiday, and I have fond memories of it from my days at the *cheder*.

"Where is it?" I asked.

"It's on Eastern Parkway in Crown Heights, a neighborhood in Brooklyn where the Lubavitch Hasidim make their home. They hold one of the greatest celebrations each year."

"Hmm . . ." I started to get a bit nervous, since I wanted to go, but not with a married man. "When I lived in Israel, I studied in a Chabad house with the Lubavitchers. Are you familiar with their movement?" Harry asked.

"I am a little," I said. "Will Rabbi Schneerson be there in person?" I was referring to the Lubavitcher Rebbe, Menachem Mendel Schneerson, who some Lubavitchers believe to be the Messiah.

"Sure, you might even get a dollar for good luck and a blessing from him," Harry answered. "That would be great, but I heard the line takes forever."

"Trust me, if you're with me, there will be no wait."

"What do you mean?" I asked, wondering if he was trying to impress me. "Just trust me," he repeated.

I couldn't hold my question in any longer, so I mustered up my courage and blurted, "First I've got to know. Are you married?"

"What?" he said, looking confused.

"The woman in the picture on your desk," I said. "I saw her." "What picture? What desk?"

"There's a picture of a woman with beautiful black hair. It's sitting on your desk in your office." "That's Harriet, my ex-girlfriend," he said.

"Current loves are displayed on desks, not exes," I huffed.

"I completely forgot about that photo. No, I'm not married, and I'm not involved with anybody.

Are we still friends?" he asked sweetly.

"Let me think about it," I said. "Okay, done. Here, you can have my phone number," I quickly replied, and scribbled my number on a small shred of napkin.

"See, I told you I would get it one day." He couldn't resist waving the napkin in my face. "I guess you were right."

"Does this mean you're coming with me to Crown Heights?" "I'm excited already."

He asked me what part of Brooklyn I lived in. "The Midwood section," I replied.

"I know that neighborhood. I worked as a taxi driver to put myself through school, and my parents still live there. I visit them often, ever since I moved to the East Side of Manhattan. I'll come and pick you up," he said, adding, "I'm really looking forward to it."

"Me too."

"If you like, how about getting together for a cup of coffee? I can show you around Manhattan," he said.

"Let's just take it one step at a time," I answered. "We'll wait and see." "We have already seen," he said, laughing to himself.

There was something about this guy that made me think he was different. He called me that very same night and we talked for nearly an hour.

The Simchat Torah celebration was quite a spectacle. People sang and danced in the streets, laughing, eating, drinking, and having a great time. Harry was attentive and kept me close at all times. He made sure that I was okay and introduced me to all of his acquaintances. Feeling a new sense of pride in my Jewishness, I dove right into the celebration.

Harry was the real thing, I could tell. He was unpretentious and his positive energy was contagious. After much rejoicing, he drove me home and we began to talk. I told him everything. I told him about my family, my childhood, life under the Communist regime, and my first unsuccessful escape attempt. I also confided in him about my successful defection to Rome, my mother's internment at Auschwitz, and her subsequent obsession with food.

I went on to tell him everything: my early years and my childhood in Porubka, my life in Kosice, my *cheder* days, my work in the pharmacy with Laura, my business ventures in Ukraine, HIAS and Ambretta in Rome, my Aunt Blanca, and school in Chicago. It was as though a floodgate had opened, and I wanted him to know the complete me. He soaked up every word. I felt so comfortable with Harry that I even told him about Sofio.

"We had some good times together but in the end we discovered that we were on different paths," I told him.

"That's understandable," Harry said. I asked him why.

"Because I cannot imagine a woman as beautiful as you being alone for long, and if not for that breakup, I wouldn't be here with you now," he said.

I had no expectations of Harry and loved that I could be completely open and honest with him. I felt safe and unguarded, as though I were talking to an old, old friend.

"Now that you've opened up, I have a confession to make," he said, smiling. "Go ahead, I'm listening."

I expected a story about a woman with three kids stashed away in Israel or a jealous ex-wife. So as to steel myself for whatever was about to come out of his mouth, I crossed my arms in front of my chest.

"The story of Harriet is not exactly as I told you," he said cautiously.

Breaking my promise to myself about never jumping to a conclusion again, I screamed, "I knew it! You men are all the same. You lie just to get your way."

"Wait a minute," he said. "Don't hold me responsible for other men's vices." "Spare me the details, I know what's next."

"Harriet wanted to get married, and I didn't. She was stunning, but somehow I knew she wasn't the right one for me. I was looking for something else in a wife."

"Like what for example?" I asked. "Someone like you," he said.

"Harriet and Harry, Sophia and Sofio . . . our stories are very similar, don't you think?" I said, and we laughed.

"Just a little bit. Perhaps we were meant to be together?" he added, with a touch of irony in his voice.

"Don't exaggerate. Did you tell Harriet that, too?" I scolded. "No. Why would you ask that?"

"Why not?" I answered.

Everything felt different with Harry. Our relationship was natural, spontaneous, and comfortable. He would plan our dates down to the minutest of details. Because of his taxi days, he was completely familiar with New York City and knew every corner, streetlight and landmark. He wanted to share it all with me. He told me that since we'd gotten together, he was no longer tired after work and couldn't wait until his shift ended. I was absolutely thrilled. Harry wanted to be with me, and I wanted to be with Harry.

I couldn't get enough of all the Middle Eastern specialty foods at his restaurant, especially the babaganoush made with charred eggplant.

I will never forget the first time I asked Harry for a plate, and expected him to go into the back for a freshly-made batch reserved for VIPs. Instead he served me directly from the display section.

"Don't you have a special batch for family and friends in the back?" I asked, incredulous, since this was common practice in Czechoslovakia.

"All my customers are my family and friends. Everyone gets the best," he answered.

I knew his actions were genuine, and he wasn't trying to impress me or anyone else. Just being in his presence, you could feel a glow radiating from inside of him. He could refresh, cool and warm your soul, all at the same time. He embodied the best qualities humanity had to offer: patience, generosity, compassion, humility, and a big heart. If someone needed to talk, he was always there to listen.

Slowly but surely, Harry embedded himself in my heart and soul, awakening every single cell in my body. We went to Broadway shows, frequented Israeli nightclubs, saw first-run movies, walked around the city, and strolled along the beaches. He also loved to buy me fresh flowers.

One time, as we were leaving a theater late at night, we saw the face of a young, vendor boy lost in a sea of balloons. Back then, it was not an uncommon sight.

"What is this little kid doing here at this hour? He should be home in his bed. Tonight, I will close down his business," Harry said, as he walked towards the boy.

"You're right. It's way past his bedtime."

"How much for the balloons?" Harry asked the boy. "Five for a buck."

"How many do you have left?" "Only these."

"Okay, I'll take them all on one condition – that you go home and get some sleep," Harry told the boy, as he handed him a wad of bills.

"Yes, sir," the boy answered, and presented me with the enormous bouquet of balloons.

My relationship with Harry deepened over time. It didn't feel like a bolt of lightning striking out of the clouds, but rather like a gentle, summer rain that envelops you in its warmth. I no longer felt like I was driving the train of life, making decisions one way or the other. Instead it felt as if life were driving me, guiding me along the path. I was merely playing my part. Together with a classmate, who also became my roommate, we moved into Manhattan and rented a two-bedroom apartment on the Upper East Side.

Harry and I celebrated my graduation from fashion design school at Windows on the World, on the 107th floor of the World Trade Center. Reservations had to be made in advance, and men were required to wear jackets. Our table was covered by a crisp white linen cloth, and we had a breathtaking view of the Manhattan skyline. Since the restaurant slowly rotated, we got to experience the city from every angle. While sipping white Italian wine, we ordered two different fish dinners. When our plates arrived, I pierced a piece of Harry's fish with my fork and said, "Let's see who ordered the better fish." It had become a regular practice for us to taste each other's meals. Taking a bite, I said, "Yours is much better."

He placed his silverware back down on the table and looked me directly in the eye.

"Since you like fish so much, how would you like to be Mrs. Fisher? You can have not only the fish on my plate, but you can also have the fish in my name."

I was so taken aback by his proposal that I couldn't think straight. "Why do you ask?" I said. "Sophia Fisher, it sounds much nicer than Sophia Manisevicova. It has a better flow."

I repeated the name over and over just to hear how it sounded. "What are you getting at?" I asked coyly.

"If you accept my proposal, I will pay much less in taxes next year," he said, obviously joking. "Since I am a fellow Jew, I would be glad to help you out," I said. "After all, what are friends for?"

Harry stood up, came around the table, and as he bent down to kiss me, he said in his typical, businesslike fashion: "Done deal."

To celebrate our sudden engagement, he ordered a bottle of the best Champagne.

I still expected that after the taxes joke, a serious marriage proposal would follow. I thought he would get down on one knee, holding a bouquet of flowers in one hand, and a diamond ring in the other. But Harry had his own way of doing things.

When the waiter returned to our table to ask if we'd like the check, Harry replied, "I already have the Czech, but I'll take the Slovak." We both burst out laughing, as the waiter stood there, looking puzzled.

The next day, as I walked into Jerusalem II, the entire restaurant broke out into cheers. "*Mazel tov!*" people shouted, as they wrapped their arms around me. Harry's brother Teddy popped open a bottle of Champagne and made a toast. Shouting over the noisy crowd, Teddy said, "*L'chaim* to my brother and his new bride!"

Harry and Teddy made a great team. While Harry was the quiet engine that hummed in the back, Teddy was the more charismatic brother. He had been born with the gift of schmooze. Harry's father known simply as

Abba, Shlomo the manager, Mario the pizza chef, and all the other workers and customers clapped and sang. Abba kept hugging me, telling me how happy he was that his last single son was getting married. "*Bubbele, meine sheine meidele*, I am so happy," he *kvelled*. Since then, he has called me nothing but.

"Me too," I said. "Not only will I gain a fantastic husband, but also a new family." "What would you like to eat?" Abba asked me.

"A slice. What else!" I said to my future father-in-law.

⨷

CHAPTER FIFTEEN

Getting Married

New York, 1981

EVERYTHING HAPPENED SO FAST, it felt like a whirlwind of activity. Within 24 hours of agreeing to "help Harry with his taxes," half of the Garment District knew about his proposal. I sat in the front of the pizzeria, grabbed my Champagne glass and, amidst all the celebrations, started to dream about our future. Where would we live? I wondered. Would we have children right away? How many would we have? What could I expect as the wife of a religious Jew? Completely immersed in my wild imaginings, I didn't even realize that I had poured sugar on my pizza instead of crushed red pepper.

Although it tasted odd, I took it as a good omen that life with Harry would always be sweet. I ate the whole piece.

Although I wanted to scream my good news from the top of the Empire State Building, instead I went to the office to call my Aunt Blanca.

"Auntie, wait, don't hang up," I said as quickly as I could.

Normally, during the week she would hang up on me, since on the weekend the phone rates were much cheaper. If it wasn't a matter of life or death, I was not supposed to call her.

"What's going on?" she asked hurriedly. "I'm getting married," I said.

"Mazel Tov!" she screamed, and this time, she didn't hang up on me. "Who? What? How?

When did this happen?" she sputtered.

"I just got engaged last night. He's an Israeli, and I know you will love him."

"Does your mother know yet?" Aunt Blanca asked. "Will she be coming to the wedding?" "I called but there was no answer. I'm going to try again now with Harry, since he speaks Yiddish. We will announce our engagement together."

"This is such wonderful news, Sophia," my aunt said. "You have made us so very happy." "I'll see you at my wedding, then. Goodbye for now."

"We wouldn't miss it for the world," she said, hanging up the phone.

As the old saying goes, good things come to those who wait. I had finally met a sweet handsome Jewish man, whom I dearly loved. I was no longer swimming against the current and what was once a fairytale, a far-away dream, had become reality. Deep in my bones, I knew that Harry would love me unconditionally. I also knew that forever and always, I would love him back.

In mid-August on Harry's 36th birthday we held our official engagement party at his family's home in Brooklyn. His parents were originally from Poland. They had fled to Kazakhstan to escape the Nazis and later emigrated to Israel.

It was during our engagement party that Harry finally bent down on one knee, just as I had hoped, and made his formal proposal. He gave me a beautiful diamond engagement ring tucked inside a white velvet box. I was constantly aware of its presence for the entire night. I simply couldn't stop looking at my finger. It was no wonder, as the stone I was wearing probably cost more than the treasured apartment I had abandoned back in Kosice. Knowing that my immigrant's dream was finally coming true, I felt a deep sense of satisfaction.

The wedding was set for that November. According to superstition, it was bad luck for a bride to make her own wedding dress. I asked Terry if one of her seamstresses could sew the dress that I had designed. I had also designed my mother's dress, which I proudly made myself. While I was busy choosing flowers, bands and catering halls, Harry was busy signing contracts and writing checks.

From the moment I first set foot on American soil, I kept in constant contact with my parents and sisters. Since I had already gotten my green card, I felt safe. Back in Kosice, everyone was doing fine – everyone except for my older sister Melanie. Due to "irreconcilable differences," she was in the process of divorcing her husband. Hanka, on the other hand, had a solid marriage. Her only complaint in life was that she felt stifled living in Czechoslovakia. Bandy, however, didn't feel the same way. He was so fanatic about his soccer league that he was willing to put up with Communist oppression for the sake of sport.

Timka was still living in Banska Bystrica, where she too had recently filed for divorce. Helga had escaped to Austria, and Laura, with her pharmacist husband Elliott, still lived close by in Brooklyn. How I wished that all of my friends and family could be with me at my wedding, sharing my joy on the biggest day of my life.

I was thrilled to find out that my parents were not only coming, but were also planning a three- month stay in New York. My mother had visited once before, when she went to see Aunt Blanca in Chicago a few years before my defection. My father, on the other hand, had never stepped foot on American soil. In fact, he had never even boarded an airplane. The night before their arrival, I was so excited that I don't think I got more than 15 minutes of sleep.

When Mother and Father stepped off the plane, my heart soared. It was such a relief to see their faces. We hugged each other at the JFK Airport arrival gate for what seemed like forever. I told them how thrilled I was to finally be getting married after all this time. Unlike Hanka and Melanie, who had married at age 21, I was already 27 years old. I knew my mother was thrilled too, as those linens she'd accumulated for my dowry could finally get some mileage.

Despite the long trip, she looked as if she had stopped off at the beauty parlor before landing in New York. Every curl was in the right place and her blouse was perfectly pressed.

Harry was standing there patiently waiting his turn to greet them.

"This is my fiancé, Harry," I said proudly, as I pushed him in front of me. "Harry, meet my parents, Simone and Yaakov Manisevic."

He gave my mother a warm hug and shook my father's hand with reverence and respect. They spoke in Yiddish as if they'd known each other their whole lives. My Israeli man endeared himself to my Czechoslovakian parents right away. This was exactly how I'd hoped it would turn out, and I was ecstatic.

My parents settled in an empty apartment in my mother-in-law's house. A week before the wedding, I moved in with them, as according to Jewish tradition the bride and groom are forbidden to see each other for seven days before the ceremony. Harry would secretly slide notes under my door or whisper to me through a key hole.

On a rainy Sunday afternoon, November 15, 1981, we got married at the

Cedarhurst Sephardic Temple on Long Island. I wanted a fairytale wedding, with crowds of people rejoicing, singing, and sharing in our good fortune. I also wanted to be the most beautiful bride in the world. Three hundred guests, most of whom I did not know, attended our wedding. Sadly, while my parents and my aunt and uncle from Chicago had been able to make it, my two sisters couldn't. But good sisters that they were, they wired me fresh flowers.

As I sat in the bridal room anxiously touching up my makeup, female guests stopped by to congratulate me, blowing kisses so as not to smudge my lipstick. My mother stood beside me, supervising as I fixed my veil and set my hair. The guests were already filling their plates with goodies from a beautifully laid out smorgasbord, the music was on, and everyone was having a good time. For some reason, though, I had an uneasy feeling that something wasn't right. It was taking too long.

Suddenly the Master of Ceremonies appeared in the bridal room to announce that the wedding had been canceled.

"What?" I almost fainted.

All of the women fell silent and the emcee asked me to accompany him to the rabbi's office. I had no clue as to what was going on. As I entered the office, I saw Harry sitting next to the rabbi, staring down at the floor, saying nothing. Had he changed his mind? Did he no longer want me?

"What is going on?" I asked, almost too scared to hear the answer.

"I forgot to bring the marriage license." Harry's voice interrupted my irrational thoughts.

The emcee was trying to calm us down. "Let your guests continue to enjoy themselves and I will explain everything to them. This has happened before and will most likely happen again, so don't worry," he reassured us.

I didn't know whether to laugh or cry. I was relieved that the reception would continue, but all the nervousness made my empty stomach cramp and I could feel tears forming under all that makeup I had spent so much time applying.

"What now?" I asked. I could tell Harry was angry at himself, fearing that he had disappointed me on my special day.

"The license is at my place back in Manhattan, but even if I broke the speed limit, in this traffic it would still take me at least three hours from Long Island and back. Without that piece of paper, our hands are tied," Harry said apologetically.

"Well, I am sure you'll understand that I cannot go against the laws of New York State," the rabbi said. "Unless there happens to be a lawyer present, the wedding cannot go on."

"One of my friends is a lawyer!" Harry shrieked.

"Excellent. Call him in here immediately so he can file an affidavit on your behalf. I am officially prohibited from pronouncing you husband and wife, so we will have to omit that sentence from the ceremony. But other than that, the wedding under the *chuppa* can go on."

The minutes that followed were frantic and chaotic, as we signed the affidavit and then ran to tell my mother that, yes, we would be getting married after all. Our guests, of course, were unaware of the drama occurring behind the scenes.

We all breathed a huge sigh of relief and a few moments later my now-contented parents held my hands as they walked me down the aisle, straight into my future.

Luckily, not one of the guests present noticed that there was no official pronouncement of "husband and wife" at the ceremony's conclusion. After Harry performed the centuries-old ritual of breaking the glass under his foot, we shared our first kiss under the *chuppa*. We were soon engulfed by many hugs, kisses, and wishes of *Mazel Tov*.

Leaving the *chuppa* hand in hand, we walked into the reception hall. Our guests joined in congratulating Mr. and Mrs. Fisher for the first time. We danced to "*Siman Tov, Mazal Tov*" until my head started to spin. The parquet floor shook under the weight of three hundred pairs of dancing shoes. As we walked to the center of the circle of our guests for our first dance, "Looking for Love in all the Wrong Places" came through the loudspeakers. Harry and I looked at each other and started to laugh. We knew our search was over.

Bidding our guests farewell shortly after midnight, we waved from the back window of a white stretch limousine and drove off to the Waldorf-Astoria Hotel to begin our honeymoon. But first we had to make a quick stop at Harry's apartment on East 38th Street to pick up our forgotten marriage license.

I had always had an idea in my head of what my husband would look like: tall, dark and handsome. But my not-so-tall Israeli man with salt-and-pepper hair surpassed all of my expectations. The next morning, with luggage packed and marriage license firmly in hand, we headed back to the rabbi's office. This time we were dressed in jeans and leather jackets.

After officially being pronounced husband and wife, we boarded a flight from JFK Airport.

We spent our honeymoon on the Caribbean island of St. Thomas. The sea was a color I had never before seen, and for the first time in my 27 years, I saw a real palm tree sprouting almost-ripe coconuts. Our luxurious hotel room was decorated with white transparent curtains that rippled in the soft Caribbean breeze. There were many varieties of richly colored flowers I hadn't even known existed. I couldn't stop taking pictures of them to later share them with my family. After dinner we would listen to live music, walk barefoot along the shore, and bask in each other's company.

Each morning I arose wishing it would never end. I thanked my grandfather Chaim and remembered the day I stood over his grave in Porubka, asking for his help. I knew beyond a shadow of a doubt that he had heard my pleas and led me to this place in my life. For one whole week the world around us ceased to exist. It was just the two of us: Mr. and Mrs. Fisher. I was a Jewish woman to my Jewish man. I was everything I always wanted to be.

CHAPTER SIXTEEN

❧

Living My Dream

New York, 1983

FINALLY, I COULD COMFORTABLY call New York my home. The city welcomed me with open arms and I thrived in its embrace. Adjusting to my new status as a married woman proved easy, and I was finally anchored in a peaceful harbor. Everything I did, I did because I wanted to. I no longer had reasons to rebel or run away to find freedom. I had become Mrs. Fisher, and I embraced my role as wife with my entire being.

The business prospered, affording Harry and Teddy the opportunity to move into a space ten times larger. The new Jerusalem II was just a block away, on Broadway between 37th and 38th Streets. Harry's little corner pizzeria wasn't so little anymore. Before we knew it, Broadway's Jerusalem II had become the largest fast food, kosher restaurant serving the finest pizza and focaccia, not to mention hummus, tahini, babaganoush, borekas, and, of course, falafel, in all of New York City.

Teddy and Harry also added their own bakery, offering a full line of freshly made kosher delights. They became renowned for their mouthwatering rugelach. Harry and Teddy sold thousands of meals a day, employed dozens of people, and their demanding business kept growing. Soon Jerusalem II was a household name in the kosher communities scattered across New York and New Jersey.

The Fisher brothers had the Midas touch: whatever they did turned to gold. For a few years, after Shabbat the mezzanine would be transformed into an Israeli nightclub with a full bar, and we'd hire famous Israeli singers for entertainment. Some of the bigger name performers to pass through our doors included Tzvika Pick, Avi Toledano, Dudu Fisher, Ron Eliron, Yoel Sharabi and Sandy Shmuely.

People from all over the New York metropolitan area flocked to Jerusalem II. They chartered buses, came by crowded subways, and drove across the George Washington Bridge just to have a taste of Harry's famous falafel balls. Our restaurant had become the place to see and be seen in the Jewish life of the city.

Whether you were an American Jew, a European Jew, or an Israeli Jew, and whether or not you adhered to kosher laws, where else in New York City would you go but Jerusalem II? The restaurant had become a beautiful shining example of the Jewish experience in New York, and especially for immigrants, it became a home away from home. By the early 1980s, it was a well-established landmark.

My new name was opening doors, and when introduced as Mrs. Harry Fisher, I was referred to as "The Wife of Jerusalem II." Here I was, this little girl from Porubka who had arrived in Rome with nothing more than a purse, a pair of underwear, about $60, and a head full of dreams, and now, just two years later, I was a respected wife and a member of a thriving Jewish community.

I embraced my new role with gusto. I never got involved in my husband's business affairs except for the rare occasion when he would ask me to help. Each Saturday, an hour after Shabbat, our place would reopen to the public and continue to be hopping until the wee hours of the morning. I would hang out with my mother-in-law, who enjoyed watching the whole scene. We had seen scores of young couples who first met at our place come back engaged, married, and finally, pushing a baby stroller. Our customers became extensions of our giant, Jerusalem II family.

Due to the ever-growing demand for our food, Teddy decided to start delivering pizzas to hungry Jews all over the world via Federal Express. And so the "New York Flying Pizza Pie" was born. Because of this innovation in pizza delivery, Broadway's Jerusalem II made it into the Guinness Book of World Records. Pizzas were sent to the dormitories of hungry students all over the world, and they would sometimes reheat them by ironing the crust on an ironing board. They were sent to newlyweds honeymooning at the Grand Canyon or families vacationing in the Caribbean. Orders regularly came in from Russia, South America, Europe, and even Asia.

One day, a Japanese comedian named Eiji Bando called and ordered a pizza to be personally delivered to his studio. The Japanese television crew decided to send Teddy on a wild goose chase. After three days of travel, 25 hours in the air with that pizza firmly placed on his lap, Teddy was sent to Los Angeles to see a sunset, then on to Honolulu to pray, and once he finally touched ground in Tokyo, he was sent by bullet train to Osaka. The Japanese television audience broke into wild applause as Teddy, yarmulke on his head, having just completing a 6,753 mile journey from New York to Osaka, hand-delivered a flying Jerusalem II kosher pizza during the live broadcast. At a total cost of $7,000, that was the most expensive pizza delivered to date.

While Harry and Teddy sold pizza, I worked in the Garment District, designing a line of junior sportswear. Wearing the basketball T-shirts I'd designed, I began to imagine my belly growing bigger and bigger, going through each and every size, from small to medium, and finally, to large. We had been planning to start a family, but first we wanted a beautiful home on the ocean. We wanted to wake up each morning to a view of white seagulls gliding over the crashing waves and watch the sunset together come evening.

Our first home was a small rental on Langham Street in Manhattan Beach, Brooklyn. Harry loved the neighborhood and kidded with me about the idea of living on a non-kosher street, since it had "ham" in the name. As it turned out, we only stayed there for a year. I set up a design studio in the basement, bought sewing machines and mannequins, and hired two seamstresses – Maria from Italy and Reina from Ecuador. I made my own designs, draped fabrics over the mannequins with pins sticking out of my mouth, developed my own patterns, and shopped for the best materials. With Maria, I practiced my Italian, and with Reina, my Spanish. I developed a full line of ready-to-wear cocktail dresses and my own label, Sophia Guffeto, was born.

In Italian, *guffeto* means little owl. I always kept Rome, Giancarlo, Ambretta and the little owl she'd brought me from Greece close to my heart. Some people collect baseball cards, refrigerator magnets, or old stamps and coins. Some even collect miniature elephants. But as for me, I collect owls. I have already amassed more than five hundred of them, ranging from pictures to ceramics to jewelry to crystal. None of my friends can look at an owl without having me pop into their heads, and a few have contributed to my ever-growing collection.

My dresses were sold in boutiques in Brooklyn, Manhattan and Long Island. The orders flooded in.

At the age of 29, my life was almost perfect, but I wanted more. The fact that my business swelled while my belly didn't bothered me to no end. At the same time, I was also becoming increasingly concerned about my sister Melanie. Mely had just gotten divorced and she was not in the greatest of moods. Speaking to her on the phone one day, I tried to calm her as much as I could.

"Hi Mely, it's me," I said, with a false cheeriness.

"Hi, how are you?" she said, sounding rather sad and defeated.

"I'm doing great. You?"

"We're hanging in there. I'm trying to make the best of this situation," she replied stoically.

Melanie was the type that kept things to herself, and she rarely let others in, including her own sisters. We were close, but I knew there was an invisible line I could never cross. I am just the opposite; I have a big mouth. When I'm down or depressed, I wear my emotions on my sleeve and my face speaks, even as my mouth stays shut. When I'm happy, it's the same way. I want to share my joy with everyone around me. But my sister had a different way of dealing with her emotions. Getting any kind of information out of her was almost impossible, and I would find myself biting my tongue. Patience, it's worth mentioning, is not one of my stronger suits. All I wanted to do was break through the walls my sister had built around herself.

"Mely, what is going on?" I said.

"I told you, nothing."

"Melanie, listen, I am here to help you. Together we can overcome anything, but if you shut me out, I cannot help you at all." I tried my best to convince her to confide in me.

Soon I began to sense her guard dropping. So as not to bother others, Melanie always took it upon herself to bear her burdens in silence, but I was determined to get her to open up. I could tell how seriously she took the failure of her marriage.

"Sophia, Mother is also very concerned about the divorce. She told me that she is upset because of it," she guiltily confided.

"Mely, our parents managed to survive the Holocaust. I'm sure one divorce won't be the end for them," I answered, hoping to reassure her.

"You've got two beautiful daughters, this marriage isn't the first Jewish marriage that didn't work out, and it's not the end of the world."

"I know, but it's very difficult for a woman trying to make it on her own with two children."

"Don't worry, men come and go, but sisters are forever. I am sure you will find someone, but until then, know that I am here for you," I said. "Listen, I have an idea. Why don't you come to the States and visit us?"

"That's easier said than done," Melanie replied, despairing.

"Mely, your girls are no longer babies. Our parents are right there, and will take good care of them.

You will have the time you need to clear your head, re-energize and see what new direction you want to take your life in."

"I don't see how this could possibly happen," she wondered aloud.

"Don't worry, we will send you a ticket and an affidavit. You will get the visa because you are only going for a visit. Since you are leaving your children behind, it is an assurance you will return. They shouldn't give you any problems."

"You know what? You're right. It makes total sense, and I could use the break," she said.

"Excellent," I replied. "I can't wait."

Within a month Melanie arrived looking exhausted, yet still quite beautiful. We had a wonderful time together, and for three weeks I took her everywhere I could. Melanie loved it in America and I naively hoped that she would meet her knight in shining armor, with a big Jewish star blazing across his helmet.

The three weeks were flying by so I kicked into high gear and began introducing her to all the available men I knew. I was hoping I could get her under the *chuppa* before her visa expired.

One thing I'd learned was that in America, you could buy anything – even a husband. But when I mentioned the possibility to Mely, she was appalled and wanted no part of it. She wanted to marry for love, she insisted. I was thrilled with my plan and expected her to react enthusiastically. But Melanie would not change her mind and at the end of three weeks she returned home alone.

Together with our real estate agent, Harry and I explored the available properties in Manhattan Beach. Eventually we found our dream house, a two-family that we would convert into a one-family, and we left the rental on Langham Street. The new house was in dire need of repair and a good dose of tender loving care. But aside from its condition, it had everything we wanted. I immediately imagined breaking down unnecessary walls, removing doors and making room for the family I hoped we would soon create.

"Shall we buy it?" Harry asked me.

"Let's go for it," I said.

The thought of owning a house in Manhattan Beach was synonymous with escaping Czechoslovakia, as each had seemed an impossible feat not too long ago. We bought the house and not long afterward, I invited my sister Hanka for a three-week visit. She got her visa with no problem, left her husband Bandy and her children behind, and came to help me prepare for our move. Finally, she arrived in New York for the first time. As I had done for Melanie, I showed her all the sights. And she also fell in love with the United States. On November 29, 1983, the day after we moved into our new home, Hanka returned to Czechoslovakia.

I was living the American Dream, but for some reason, my belly still wasn't growing. The years were flying by and my clock began to tick louder and louder. I began to wonder whether there might be a fertility problem. The thought that for some unknown reason we would be unable to have children felt like a harsh and undeserved sentence. Each month, when I realized that I wasn't pregnant my heart would sink once again. As I walked down the street, my head would turn to look at every baby carriage that passed me by. I dreamed that one day I too would be pushing my own baby in a carriage.

To celebrate my thirtieth birthday in January, Harry surprised me with tickets to Las Vegas. I was taken aback not just by all the lights, noise, and people throwing money around as though it meant nothing, but also by how it felt like a playground made for adults. It was open 24 hours a day, seven days a week. While in Las Vegas, I tried to drag Harry away from the gambling tables. But he was stubborn, jumping from roulette to Blackjack and all the different poker tables, trying to push his luck. As I looked down, I realized I had lost the gold bracelet Harry had given me earlier that day for my birthday. I was devastated, as I had put it on just hours before.

"Don't worry, my love, I will buy you a nicer one," he whispered into my ear at the blackjack table. He had such a way with words that no matter how upset I would get, he could always comfort me.

Since I had never been bitten by the gambling bug, I decided to explore

Caesar's Palace on my own. In the ladies' room, I was confronted by an old Gypsy woman.

"Lady, let me read your palm," she demanded, as she used her body to block my exit from the restroom. "Only $10."

Since I wasn't in the best mood after losing my bracelet and I had no previous experience with fortune tellers, I took her up on the offer.

She pushed me a little farther into the corner of the restroom, grabbed my hand, placed it in hers, turned my palm up and carefully studied each line. She then looked at me, back at my hand again, back at me once more, and with an air of sophistication, said, "Madam, within a year you will give birth to a son. Believe me lady, a great future awaits you." She was smiling as she said it.

I laughed as I placed a $100 bill into her wrinkled palm and closed her fingers around it. When she opened her hand, she was so shocked that she exclaimed, "Thank you, lady. It is going to happen, mark my words!"

Shortly after our return to New York, the doctor confirmed that I was indeed expecting a baby.

Months before I was showing, I began to shop for and wear maternity clothes. But because of the Jewish belief that life does not begin until the moment of birth, I refrained from buying baby clothes. Instead I would window shop, making mental notes of what I would buy from each store as soon as my baby arrived.

On October 16, 1984, my first son, Henry Chaim Fisher, was born. Overjoyed that their baby finally had her baby, my parents came for a six-month visit. We were all ecstatic at his birth, none more so than Harry. He immediately began planning his son's *brit milah*, or ritual circumcision, but instead of holding it in a synagogue, he preferred to hold the ceremony for this great mitzvah in our home.

I had fulfilled the promise I had made at my grandfather's grave in Porubka, following my first unsuccessful escape attempt. Henry's Hebrew name was Chaim. For the *brit milah*, Harry had all the food catered by Jerusalem II, with specialty dishes prepared just for the occasion. Scores of people attended and I officially became the newest member of another community – this time it was the community of mothers.

That old Gypsy fortune teller had been right.

Sadly, Hanka and her family couldn't make it in time for the *brit milah*. But she had a good reason. Together with her husband Bandy and their children Emma and Artur, Hanka had fled Czechoslovakia via Yugoslavia.

A month or so later, on November 29, 1984 – exactly one year minus a day since returning home from her previous visit to New York – she arrived with her family and Harry and I welcomed them to America, their new home.

We had known nothing of their escape plans. My brother-in-law, an accomplished A-league soccer referee, had not been accepted into the international ranks and he believed it was solely because he was Jewish. So he hung up his soccer shoes, whistle, and uniform, and without any hesitation or drama, he packed his belongings and his family into the car and drove to Yugoslavia using the guise of a summer vacation.

After their safe arrival in Belgrade, Bandy went to the UN office and applied for political asylum in the United States. For the next four months, the whole family was taken care of by the UN and the local Jewish community. In order to make extra money and knowing they would no longer have any use for a car, they sold it for spare parts.

Before I had the chance to take another breath, I was expecting my second baby. On October 31, 1985 I gave birth to a boy named David Eliezer. The Las Vegas Gypsy's predictions proved to be worth their weight in gold. I had Harry, my mother, father, and Hanka and her family all around me. Bandy and Hanka soon found employment, their children were enrolled in school, and before long, they were able to stand on their own two feet.

Not long afterward, Harry and Teddy acquired another restaurant across the street from Broadway's Jerusalem II. The restaurant, called R. Gross, was renowned for its blintzes. We converted it into a Middle Eastern restaurant, serving meat specialties, and named it Chez Lanu. Slowly we began adding other Jewish-American specialties, and before long, Chez Lanu became Mr. Broadway Delicatessen. It was not only a deli, but also served kosher Asian food. Mr. Broadway and Jerusalem II are still located in the heart of Manhattan near Macy's, the Empire State Building, Madison Square Garden, and Times Square.

With the help of a great PR agent, the business became even more successful.

"Darling, are you ready for your close up?" Harry asked me one day.

He had just returned home from work, and as usual, he gave me a kiss and ran to play with the kids.

"Excuse me?" I said.

"We received an offer to appear on the Regis and Kathie Lee show."

"You must be kidding! I watch them every morning with my coffee." As Henry crawled between his legs, he held David in his arms. "What am I supposed to do on there?" I asked, confused.

"They want you to appear in their cooking segment."

"Forget it," I said stubbornly.

"Come on, darling," he said, and laughed at my overreaction.

"And when is this supposed to happen?"

"The morning before Passover is the day they chose. They want you to prepare potato latkes with matzo meal from scratch."

"Harry, I think you should ask your chef instead, as hers are so much more delicious."

"Between you and me, I prefer yours. Sophia, this is ABC national television. I mean, it's Regis Philbin and Kathie Lee Gifford's morning show. Do it for our business! Besides, you are such a beautiful woman, let them have two good things to watch."

"For you, Harry, I'd do anything. Tell them it's a done deal."

Together, we went over the details and ingredients of the recipe. I prepared the latkes every single day for the next two weeks and worked on my accent holding my round hairbrush as a microphone in front of the mirror. I tried on every outfit in my closet and styled my hair every which way so as to look perfect. I felt as if I were preparing for my Hollywood debut.

"Harry, I'm terrified that I'll get stage fright and I won't be able to speak. What if I look awful on camera?"

"Sophia, you could walk into that studio in the sack that the potatoes came in and still take my breath away."

A month later I walked into the television studio in a brand new lace-trimmed suit. My hair and makeup were done by the professional stylists. On set, I dug my neatly-manicured nails into the batter, added marjoram, my mother's secret ingredient, and did my best to introduce the secret of Mother's latkes to the American audience. Regis made me feel so comfortable on set that I couldn't thank him enough after the segment.

Harry was the most attentive father in the world. He cuddled our boys in his arms for hours, sang Jewish melodies as he gently rocked them to sleep, and always gave them a kiss on the forehead before placing them already asleep in their beds. Nothing is more attractive than a man who can express his love and compassion to his own children. There was never a time when I was placed in a position of having to choose sides between the boys and Harry. We were one.

I adopted the lifestyle of the traditional, yet modern, American Jewish woman. As the owners of one the most popular kosher restaurants in New York, our social circle in the religious community expanded, and the more I learned, the more observant I became. I began attending seminars and classes so I could better familiarize myself with Jewish customs, traditions, holidays, rituals, and history. We even sent our children to the local yeshiva.

CHAPTER SEVENTEEN

࿖

Traveling to Israel and Italy

S HORTLY AFTER OUR WEDDING and long before our boys were born,
Harry and I took our first trip to Israel together. He introduced me
to the rest of his family and showed me beloved places from his
childhood. Just being there helped me to answer many of the questions
I'd held inside for so long. To my surprise, life in Israel was much more
normal than I'd been taught as a child. I learned from this experience the
important lesson that I should get my facts straight and never listen to
conjecture.

Harry had grown up in the ancient city of Jaffa, considered one of the
oldest ports in the world. Jaffa was supposedly named after one of Noah's
sons, Jafet, who was instructed to build the city forty years after the biblical
flood. We visited Harry's family home, stopped by the Chabad House in a
moshav, revisited Harry's old Lubavitcher Yeshiva, and then stopped by to
see friends he'd left behind after his bar mitzvah. Everybody remembered
my mother-in-law, who walked into the synagogue with perfect posture
each Shabbat, as well as my father-in-law and their three sons.

It is said that once a Jew makes that first trip to Israel it becomes his
or her home forever – even without deciding to move there. I fell in love
with Tel Aviv, a modern city, as well as with Eilat, a Red Sea resort town
on the Gulf of Aqaba. During the exodus from Egypt, Eilat was one of the
stations the Israelites crossed on their way to the Holy Land, and it was
later conquered by King David.

Harry and I enjoyed ourselves immensely and with every step I took,
the visit grew in meaning and significance. I felt as if my own feet were
tracing the path of my ancestors. Thanks to Harry, as well as my father's
Shabbat stories from my childhood, Jewish history became more tangible

than I had ever imagined. It was in Jerusalem that Harry and I vowed that if ever we had a son, his bar mitzvah would take place right there.

Jerusalem was destroyed twice, besieged 23 times, conquered 44 times, and attacked 55 times. Yet it still stands proud and strong. When I went to the women's side of the Western Wall, I inserted a rolled-up piece of paper with my prayers between the cracks of the ancient stones. As I pushed my wish deeply into the wall, knowing it would be fulfilled, I cried. Meanwhile, Harry stood on the men's side, pushing his own prayers into the *Kotel*, as this wall is called.

When it came to visiting the Yad Vashem Holocaust memorial museum, I had conflicting feelings. On one hand, I found it depressing to hear the same stories repeated over and over through the decades. But on the other hand, I also knew that those who choose to forget history are doomed to repeat it. Looking at the countless photographs, drawings and documents of the atrocities committed against my fellow Jews, I almost fainted. Then, as I noticed a charcoal drawing of the brick factory ghetto in Kosice, I burst into uncontrollable sobs. This mesmerizing piece of art, hanging in front of my eyes, had been drawn by none other than Ludovit Feld, my dear Uncle Lajos.

"Harry, look!" I squealed, squeezing his arm. "This was made by my art teacher who still lives in Kosice."

"You see, darling, every Jew, no matter where they come from, has roots here. You have found yours." Once again, Harry performed his own personal brand of magic by finding the perfect words to soothe my aching soul. As our trip wound down and we packed our bags to head home, a light bulb went off in my head.

"Harry, since we are not far from Europe, why not stop in Rome on the way back?" I suggested.

"Excellent idea, since we have a few days left. I'll call the airline and make hotel reservations in Rome."

Visiting not just Israel but Rome as well, before going home to New York was an unexpected treat. I was ecstatic. We decided to call the trip our second honeymoon, since with Harry everything always came in pairs. We got married twice, later had two sons, and celebrated my birthday twice each year – my real one, as well as the day I finally made it to America. I had two homelands – Slovakia and Italy – and so did Harry – Israel and America. I had two sisters and he had two brothers.

It did not occur to us that in addition to my passport I also needed a visa, since I was not yet an official American citizen. Much to my disappointment, I was prohibited from entering the country when we reached Leonardo DaVinci airport. I don't know why I was under the impression that it would be easy.

Given my history with border crossings, I should have known better.

"No problem, we'll return another time. I'll change the connecting flight back to New York and we'll head home," Harry said, as he gently tried to steer me away.

"Just give me a minute to think," I said, since I was never one to give up before I had explored all my options. I also knew that Italians had a soft spot for romantic love stories.

In fluent Italian, I asked the officer if he would be so kind as to let me speak with his superior. As I was shown into the office, I tried to explain to the high-ranking official the reason why I wanted to go to Rome, even if just for 24 hours.

"I have no intention of remaining in Italy illegally," I said. "I wish more than anything to reunite with the family that helped me defect from Czechoslovakia, and I would like to introduce them to my new husband. They are here right now, waiting outside for us."

I called Harry in to join us, and the chief officer asked him some additional questions. He checked his passport and within minutes I was holding a transit permit for a 48-hour stay in Italy. I hugged the customs officer and thanked him profusely as we left to greet the "Italian branch" of our extended family. Two days later, as we awaited our flight back to New York, that same officer found a bottle of fine Champagne on his desk and a thank-you note from the newlyweds.

Outside, there was a lively crowd of people waiting for us. We hugged and kissed each other endlessly, and for the next two days and nights, we stuffed our faces as if there was no tomorrow.

"Brava Sophia, you look radiant," Ambretta said, upon seeing me.

"That's exactly how I feel," I told her. "Harry and I are truly happy together. It happened as if it were preordained, and I feel so fortunate to have a husband like him. The only regret I have is that he doesn't speak Italian, so you can really get to know him. Ambretta, I know Giancarlo has a fear of flying, but you must come to New York to visit us and bring your daughter, too. I hope that will be the next time we see each other."

"I wish it were so, but I have the same fear of flying as my brother. But

I am sure that Vanessa wouldn't think twice," Ambretta said, hugging and kissing me, as Italians tend to do.

In the city, Harry and I made a point of stopping by and visiting Matylda at the HIAS office. She was nicely dressed as usual, still working at the same desk and helping to resettle Jews from around the world. Not much had changed in three years, including the sounds of the chaotic streets. The only difference was that everything looked slightly smaller than when I first walked through the doors of HIAS. Harry had already settled my bill with them long ago, but on this day he also promised another generous donation. We believed, as the saying goes, that "If you save one life, you save an entire nation."

CHAPTER EIGHTEEN

ૐ

Homecoming

Czechoslovakia, USA, 1987

D URING THE PASSOVER HOLIDAYS in 1987, I returned to Kosice for the first time since my defection. I could hardly wait. By now I had my official American citizenship – the naturalization process had taken forever but eventually went off without a hitch. I was excited to share my old home with my new family.

Dragging eight huge suitcases, Harry, our two sons, and I with my new American passport, traveled together to Czechoslovakia. I treated my homecoming extravagantly and brought gifts for everyone I knew. For Melanie I brought a designer leather coat, and for the rest of the family I brought t-shirts, cosmetics, costume jewelry, and all kinds of inexpensive items from Chinatown, bought by the dozen. There was enough to go around for everyone I encountered.

The first reason for my return, besides reuniting with my family, was to prove to myself that everything I had endured was worth it. The second reason was to take care of my sister Melanie and my two nieces. Although she never complained, I knew she missed me dearly and appreciated my support. The third reason was to see Ludovit Feld once again and introduce him to Harry.

Harry fell in love with the city of Kosice and took to it immediately. Since Americans rarely peeked behind the Iron Curtain, we became the talk of the town. I was so happy to see my sister again and I could tell how proud and joyous they were for me, especially Mely. But beneath her smile, I sensed remorse and sadness as we began to talk.

"I should have listened to you," she cried in our parent's kitchen. It felt as if we had turned back into the little girls we once were.

Since Mely was now divorced, she felt solely responsible for her daughters' upbringing. Ingrid, her firstborn – and a rabble-rouser, like me – had fallen in love with a non-Jew and wanted to get married. Mely told me she had tried everything possible to break them up but nothing seemed to work.

"Don't worry, we'll figure something out," I said in an effort to appease her. I offered her a cup of freshly-brewed coffee to help calm her nerves.

Now I could better understand my parents' restriction against marrying outside the faith. We all tried to talk Ingrid out of it to no avail. Like a typical young woman, smitten by the love bug for the first time, she was steadfast in her conviction. Deep down I wasn't quite ready to accept that my niece would marry outside of our religion and compromise the bloodline.

"I will get her to America," I promised Melanie.

"I would be so grateful," she said, sighing with relief.

Unknown to us, Ingrid had entered her grandmother's home. We were so engrossed in our conversation that we hadn't even noticed when she walked in.

"Don't you get it? I know what I want!" Ingrid shouted.

"What do you think you are doing, eavesdropping on a private conversation?" Melanie admonished.

"Mother, come on. You take everything way too seriously," my niece said.

"Just you wait. When you become a mother, you'll understand," Mely replied, sounding just like our mother.

"Relax, Mom. In case you haven't noticed, I'm already an adult and I know what I want. You have to let me live my own life."

"No one is telling you what to do, Ingrid. I know what being in love for the first time is like," I said, trying to mediate the situation.

"So?" she replied.

I decided at that moment that the best way to help Mely would be to take care of Ingrid. I also liked the idea of having more of my family around me in Brooklyn.

"Why don't you do what I did and visit New York for two weeks before you reach a final decision about tying the knot?" I asked Ingrid.

"I've heard that before. Two weeks will turn into two years and who knows how long after that?

You will keep me stuck in your house setting me up with every available Jewish man, and all the while I'll be miserable."

"Ingrid, this is New York City," I said. "There is so much more to see than just men. I respect your wishes and I don't want you there just for a *shidduch*, an arranged marriage."

"Whether you like it or not, agree or disagree, I am not going anywhere. I like it here." Ingrid slammed the door behind her as she left.

"Wait a minute!" Mely shouted.

"Mom, enough, I'll see you later," she shouted back. Then she poked her head into the room one last time, before she stomped out to do whatever she pleased.

"Don't panic, I'll make it happen," I said, trying to calm my sister down. "Before you know it, this too shall pass, and you will soon be dancing at her wedding in Brooklyn. I'll make sure she forgets about her boyfriend. Wait and see. Harry and I will look after Ingrid ourselves, so you have nothing to worry about".

"I don't know if I can do that." Mely started to cry.

"Stop crying. Enough feeling sorry for yourself. Remember what Mother told us – that unless you have truly suffered, you will never understand real pain."

"Yes, I remember," she said. I could feel her resistance waning.

"Before you know it, Ingrid will come around, and you and Darinka will travel to your firstborn's wedding," I said, smiling at her.

"How can you be so sure?"

"It's in my Gypsy blood," I said, as I winked at my sister.

"I certainly hope so," she said.

The difference between Ingrid and me was that my life's goal was to go to America in search of a better life. I pursued that goal with intense passion and determination. Ingrid possessed the same qualities and was determined to follow her heart, but unlike me, she was most concerned with attaining freedom from her mother's "outdated" rules. I, on the other hand, was most concerned with attaining freedom from the oppressive rules of religion and escaping Czechoslovakia. My niece was also a rebel, but for different reasons.

Together with Harry and Maximilian Bush, we went to visit the artist Ludovit Feld at his small apartment in Kosice. I couldn't wait to see him again. At 83 years old, with diminished eyesight and equal in size to my two-year-old son, Uncle Lajos was sitting alone in the semi-darkness of his tiny apartment. He greeted us with a smile.

"Despite the fact that I can't see so well anymore, I am so happy that you came," he said in his unforgettable voice. It sounded as if he had inhaled helium from a balloon.

"What an honor and a joy to see you again, Uncle Lajos. I would like to introduce you to my husband Harry," I said, excitedly.

Immediately Harry began asking endless questions, and Feld responded to each one, searching for the correct expressions, occasionally stopping to find just the right words. I translated the entire conversation and explained to him that Harry was an active member of the Holocaust Memorial Committee in Sheepshead Bay, Brooklyn. We videotaped the entire visit and hung on every word that came from Feld's lips.

Everything in his miniature apartment was adjusted for his height. I noticed that very few of his paintings hung on the walls. The windows were covered by heavy curtains that the sun's rays could not penetrate. Outside it was spring, but inside Uncle Lajos' dark spare apartment it felt like autumn – the autumn of his life.

"Maestro Feld, I would like to purchase some of your art. I admire your work greatly and would like to own some more of your pieces," my husband said.

"I only have a few left and am not sure I want to part with them," replied Uncle Lajos.

"I respect that. If I can be of assistance in any way, please do not hesitate to ask," Harry said, expressing his natural warmth and compassion.

"I feel that sooner rather than later I will be gone," Feld said. "I know my days are numbered, but there is one thing I still wish for. I'm not sure if you can help me with this matter, though. Before my days are over, I would like to see the surviving twins who I lived with in the barracks, especially Kalman."

"Are you referring to Kalman Bar-On?" Harry asked.

"Yes. He was like the son I never had. We shared a bunk and spooned to keep warm. The most important thing is that he survived, and is alive and well. To see him one more time would mean the world to me. I would also like to know what became of that fidgety little boy, Pepiczek. I would paint him every day to cheer him up and calm his fears. Then I can die in peace."

139

"Life is unpredictable. You never know what tomorrow might bring," Harry answered.

"Sophia, are you still painting?" Uncle Lajos asked, changing the subject.

"No, I am not at the moment. I have two young sons but that dormant artist in me has been revived. Now I am designing dresses," I said. "My creative side is still alive and well," I added, hoping to make him proud.

"That makes me happy," he said, and rewarded me with the sweet smile I'd missed for so long.

Finally, we prepared to say our last good-byes to Ludovit Feld. We didn't pressure him for any more information. Right then and there, a seed was planted. One day, I thought, I will arrange an exhibition of his work at an art gallery, or perhaps even a museum.

"I am so deeply touched and relieved to see you again," I told dear Uncle Lajos. "I will cherish this moment forever." Harry nodded his head in agreement.

"You too, take good care my dear friends," he said in parting. This was the last time we ever saw him again.

When we left the apartment, Bush could not contain his excitement. As we got into his car, he said,

"Allow me, please, to take you to my place. I have something I think you might be interested in."

"Gladly," my husband said, accepting his offer.

We thought that he would introduce us to Mrs. Bush, whom I adored, and I couldn't wait to embrace her once again. I was looking forward to making the introduction when Bush's wife, Irena, appeared at the front door. I remembered how I had visited her often, helping her with chores, and how she would always give me a treat afterward. Irena, whom I still called Manci, invited us inside. We sat on the sofa and she served us tea in her famous pink porcelain tea set from Carlsbad, along with biscuits dipped in chocolate.

"I am so happy to see you again," she shrieked, her hair freshly permed and her unmistakable Hungarian accent fully intact.

Manci had aged over the years, but she still retained that unique sense of humor that I loved so much. As we drank our tea, Bushinko stood up and pushed a heavy armoire away from a wall, revealing a secret hiding place. There, between the wall and the armoire, he had stored Feld's original drawings for nearly forty years. They were the exact same pieces that Feld had rewarded him with for letting him use his studio after World War II. Fortunately we were able to acquire Feld's paintings from Bushinko right there on the spot. They were priceless treasures and Harry didn't hesitate to offer him quite a nice sum.

"Six million cannot speak. The rest of the world *must* see their suffering," Harry said, obviously moved by the scenes portrayed in the charcoal drawings.

It was enough for Bushinko, who proceeded to tenderly seal them back between the two pieces of plywood that had been their sanctuary for so long. After that, we all went back to drink our tea in Manci's pink porcelain cups.

One of our newly acquired gems was drawn in 1944. Feld had used charcoal to portray a scene called *The Funeral*, which he'd drawn inside the Kosice brick factory a *de facto* ghetto. The second drawing, titled *Father and Son*, was painted from memory after liberation in 1948. Against the backdrop of the crematoria smokestacks in Auschwitz, a boy leans weakly upon his father. He appears to be a victim of Mengele's deranged experiments, and both of their faces are etched in anguish.

Feld's paintings carried a profound message and emotional weight that anyone, art lover or not, could recognize. Upon our return to New York, I showed the drawings to my Hungarian neighbor who immediately began to cry. When she regained her composure, she sighed. "I know this place quite well," she said.

"You mean the ghetto?" I asked her.

"Yes. I was there in Teglagyar as well," she said, pointing at the brick factory.

Years later, while visiting Israel in the spring of 2010, I arranged a personal meeting with Kalman Bar-On at his apartment. Since the war, he had never left Israel. He greeted me cordially, as he began to recount the story of his internment in Auschwitz and his memories of the time he spent with Ludovit Feld and Pepiczek.

It had taken 44 years for Feld, Kalman and Pepiczek, accompanied by Israeli author and politician Yossi Sarid, to finally reunite. In the fall of 1989, the three men traveled from Israel to Kosice, only to find a ravished Feld in a hospital bed, looking like a rag doll and nearing the end of his life. Kalman Bar-On's story has been published in many books in which he frequently referred to his distant relative Ludovit Feld.

"He was bedridden and frail, and I became overwhelmed with emotion at this gift of seeing him once more," Bar-On told me. "Although we didn't say much, the three of us held hands the entire time. As tears streamed down his cheeks, Peter Grunfeld, known as Pepiczek, kneeled down and placed the old man's hand on his face, so he could feel the features of the four-year-old boy he had painted so precisely and intimately," Bar-On continued.

"'I am okay, Uncle Lajos, and so happy to be here with you,' Peter cried."

"I was hoping I would have the chance to be reunited with you one more time. Unfortunately I can't see your faces anymore, but just like all those faces in Auschwitz I painted, they are deeply etched in my memory for eternity. All the drawings I did of Dr. Mengele from the camp, which I was forced to do more times than I can remember, he confiscated. I drew him so many times I could do it from memory. I must confess a secret to you now that no one else knows. Since the liberation, I never again drew his portrait, not even once. That is *my* revenge," Feld explained.

Later on, Bar-On described his final moments with Feld, down to the last detail. "Uncle Lajos was much older than me, and although the age difference was vast, he was the father figure. But because of my height, I was the adult. I would stand on the food lines for him, because he had a fear of being trampled and pushed, as he was so small he couldn't even reach up for his serving. I brought him his tea and portion of bread and scoop of soup each day," Bar-On recounted.

"He rarely expressed himself with words, mostly through his art. I am so happy he lived long enough to see you again," I told Bar-On. "Your relationship meant so much to him."

"And for us, it meant so much to see that he had returned to his Jewish roots. He wanted us to know that he had been studying *Tanach*, Bible, and lighting the Shabbat candles."

For Feld, their meeting also meant that he was finally free to liberate himself from his earthly body and his gruesome memories. I took as many notes as I could so that one day I would be able to introduce Feld to the world through the eyes of those who loved him. Ludovit Feld died in Kosice on May 18, 1991. He is buried there in the same Jewish cemetery as my parents.

Upon my return from Kosice, I began working on fulfilling the promise I had made to my sister Melanie about getting her daughter Ingrid to New York. Much to my surprise, our invitation was immediately accepted. We met Ingrid at JFK Airport in the summer of 1988. On the drive home, I asked her what had happened that had changed her mind so quickly.

"A book," she told me.

"What book?" I asked.

"A book I never read. Let me explain. I work as a librarian in the city's Scientific Library. As you recall, the dilapidated synagogue on Zvonarska Street between Gates #5 and #7 had been used as a warehouse for our old outdated books." I nodded as she continued to speak. "One fateful morning I was driven there with five of my colleagues in a van filled with more old books to be stored away. We created a human chain, passing each book from the person in the van to the next in the line, until the book went through all of our hands on its way to the depository. At one point one of my colleagues said in a mysterious voice, 'They are going to come out soon,' as if aliens had just landed on earth right next to us. She continued on in that same, disturbing voice, 'Look! Here they come, The Jews . . .'"

Before she was able to finish her sentence, Ingrid looked up and saw her own grandfather exiting the shul. Without saying a word their eyes locked, and in silence, they communicated with each other, standing a mere three feet apart. He acknowledged her position, and not wanting to reveal her identity and subject her to verbal abuse, he motioned with his eyes to stay put and went on his way without another glance or word.

"I stood in my spot as if frozen to the ground," Ingrid said. "Holding the last book from the van, I realized that this was no longer a book, but the final straw that broke the camel's back. I knew right then and there that I could no longer live where I was unable to be myself or have the freedom to run into my adoring grandfather's arms. After my shift ended, I went to my grandparents' house and sobbed uncontrollably. I felt as if I had no choice but to accept your offer for the two-week visit. So here I am."

I make no claims of being a prophet but my premonition that my niece would end up permanently in the United States proved correct. Ingrid fell in love with New York, and later on, with a young eligible bachelor named Joey, who also happened to be Jewish. Her Kosice affair became a distant memory, and soon we were in the midst of preparing an engagement party for the happy couple.

After setting the date, Ingrid and Joey immediately made arrangements for Melanie and Darinka to travel to Brooklyn for the nuptials. Two weeks turned into forever for Ingrid, and Melanie and Darinka also decided to stay in Brooklyn. What a sight it was. As Ingrid stood beneath the *chuppa* with her groom surrounded by our entire family, my once rebellious niece was beaming. Our family's journey, even the awful parts, had paid off, since here we were all standing together in Brooklyn, at last.

CHAPTER NINETEEN

Why Is This Happening?

New York, 1989

WORKING IN THE RESTAURANT BUSINESS made for a difficult and demanding life. Harry had to be a jack- of-all-trades, always on call, ready to help his employees whenever he was needed. Being a successful business owner didn't necessarily mean living high on the hog, collecting huge profits. It meant being awake when everyone else was asleep, missing dinners at home, filling in for sick employees, and working harder than the entire staff combined. Harry respected every single one of his employees and considered them his extended family. He loved his work and was always full of zest and energy, until one day everything changed.

When Harry was a young boy growing up in Israel, he contracted rheumatic fever and developed a slight heart murmur. This is a common condition, and Harry was always under the care of his physician. In 1989 the restaurants were growing rapidly and we were remodeling our house. Our two sons were enrolled in the preschool of the Yeshiva of Manhattan Beach. We had also found a great nanny, Yolanda, who lived with us. Our sons David and Henry called her Ganga and she adored them.

My life as Mrs. Fisher suited me perfectly and I was happier than I'd ever imagined was possible. My day started with the obligatory cup of coffee and cigarette – a habit I had yet to break – and I felt great. However, we never know what fate has in store for us. There is an old Yiddish saying, "Man makes plans and God laughs."

In September 1989 my life changed forever. I always tried to live according to the wisdom of my beloved Harry, whose favorite saying was, "Live and let live." My parents also taught us from an early age to "Always look after others before yourself." I had been soaking in the sweet aromas of life, going through its trials and tribulations, never expecting an upheaval of such magnitude.

In mid-August, right around Harry's 44th birthday, we went on a long-awaited summer vacation to Europe. When we returned a week later, Harry immediately switched back into work mode. Not long after we landed, he rushed to both restaurants to make sure everything was running smoothly. Ganga took our boys to the beach and I had the entire house to myself. As I unpacked our luggage, listening to Fleetwood Mac, I suddenly realized that Harry had returned home looking pale as a ghost.

At first I wasn't alarmed. I assumed it was due to jet lag and felt certain that within a day or two his body would acclimate to the time change. How wrong I was. Harry's condition worsened and before long he was getting paler and warmer by the minute. He had developed a fever and chills. When he didn't go to work Saturday evening, I knew that his condition had nothing to do with the weather or jet lag. The following day we were invited to the wedding of our friends' daughter at the Pierre Hotel in Manhattan. I had been looking forward to the wedding all week.

"Darling, how do you feel?" I asked Harry.

"I'm fine. Just a little tired, that's all. Don't worry, it will be out of my system soon enough." My darling Harry never complained.

"You still look pale," I said.

"It's nothing. I told you I feel fine."

"You don't look fine to me," I countered. "Forget about the wedding. It will happen whether we are there or not. Go and lie down. You look like you haven't slept all night and your face is burning up. I'll make you some tea."

"Drinking hot tea in the summer? Forget about the tea. Go and put on that beautiful dress you bought in Vienna. And hurry up, I can't wait to see you in it."

The dress was hanging in the closet near my black high heels, Harry's dark suit, snow white shirt, and a blue pinstriped tie. It was a fantastic combination. But when I got to the bedroom, I secretly dialed his cardiologist.

"Hello, this is Sophia Fisher, Harry's wife," I said in a hushed tone.

"How can I help you, Mrs. Fisher?" he asked.

"Doctor Feder, I am extremely concerned about Harry. He is very pale and has had sweats and chills all night. At first, I thought it might be due to jet lag, since we just returned from Europe, but he's been running a fever ever since. He claims that there's nothing to worry about, but I disagree," I said, all in one single breath.

"I can't make a diagnosis over the phone, but perhaps he's just stressed out. In any case, since he's under my watch and it is Labor Day Weekend, I'll meet you at the emergency room at Maimonides Hospital as soon as possible. Let's give him a checkup to make sure we haven't neglected anything," the doctor said calmly.

"Neglected, what do you mean?" I asked.

"Harry suffers from a heart murmur, which can put him at a higher risk for infection. I'd like to see him immediately," the doctor said.

"We're on our way."

Instead of wearing my beautiful Viennese dress, I entered the kitchen dressed in jeans and a T-shirt as Harry waited for his tea to cool down. He didn't expect to see me dressed like that and, forgetting about the tea, he made his way into the living room. I found him sitting on the sofa wrapped in a blanket, shivering from chills. His eyes were watery and his head felt like it was on fire.

"I just spoke with your cardiologist," I informed my husband.

"Why?"

"Because you're sick and I'm getting sick from worry. Dr. Feder agreed with me and would like to see you immediately. I am not going to any wedding until I'm sure that everything is okay."

Under ordinary circumstances, my husband would challenge me, as he had a bit of a stubborn streak in him. He might accuse me of exaggerating, or blowing things out of proportion, but not this time. Harry simply stood up and with a nod of his head indicated that he agreed with me. I sensed deep in my gut that this was something serious. I felt as if a dark cloud were hovering over me, and an electric charge surged through my body causing me to jump. I put on my sunglasses, grabbed both the house and the car keys, and prepared to leave.

Then Harry quietly said, "You stay home with the children. I will drive myself."

I noticed that he was staggering around the kitchen. His eyes were bloodshot and glazed, and he seemed confused. "Not a chance," I said. "I'm going with you, but you can drive if you insist." I didn't want him to

147

drive, but I also didn't want to argue with him and risk losing any more time.

I was extremely anxious the whole way to the hospital. I wished the traffic would speed up and the traffic lights would change color more quickly. By the time we arrived at the Maimonides Hospital emergency room, Harry was short of breath. A cardiologist was already there waiting for us. He took one look at Harry and immediately recognized that his condition was serious. Harry was admitted to the hospital right then and there.

As I stood waiting in the hallway, my mind raced. I called my mother-in-law, Harry's brothers, Teddy and Dan, and my two sisters. My calls were straightforward and to the point: we were in the hospital and it was serious, I said. All of Harry's family showed up at practically the same time and we greeted each other solemnly, without any drama. At the age of 35, I felt as if my own life force was being sapped along with my husband's.

"Mrs. Fisher?" a doctor asked, as he approached us in the waiting room.

"Right here!" I jumped out of my chair.

"Your husband is suffering from sub-acute bacterial endocarditis and needs immediate surgery. "

"What?" I cried in disbelief.

"It's a very serious condition that can have severe effects on the heart," he said.

"But do you have to operate on his heart?"

"Yes."

The doctor's words rang in my ears. I could barely pay attention to what he was saying. All I could hear was heart surgery, surgery, right away, heart, immediate.

"How did this come about? He's always been so strong and healthy" I asked, bewildered.

"Because of rheumatic heart fever, patients such as Harry belong to a very high risk group. At first, the symptoms may appear innocent, more like a regular flu or cold, but the difference is that they don't get better. The bacteria attack the heart's inner tissue directly through the bloodstream," the doctor explained.

We were all in shock. Life can change in a split second.

"Come to think of it, we were about to attend a wedding. Just minutes ago, he was telling me not to worry . . ."

I stopped, unable to continue as I thought of our recent trip through

Europe. Suddenly the vacation and all the giggling happy children building sandcastles on the beach felt like a distant memory.

"I don't want to offer you any false hope, or jump to hasty conclusions. However, I have to say, in all honesty, that his condition is serious," the doctor continued.

"How serious?" we all asked in unison.

"It is quite serious, indeed."

"You mean . . ." I couldn't continue.

"Yes, critical."

"Oh, my God . . ."

"It's his heart, after all," the doctor went on.

"What can you do about it? Can you help him now? There has to be something!" He must have heard the desperation in my voice.

"First, we must reduce his temperature. After that, we will re-examine his heart and then decide what our next course of action will be."

"I must see him now," I said, as I started to run towards his room.

"Go ahead, Mrs. Fisher. I'm sure he would be happy to see you, too."

At that moment, even after all I'd been through in my life, I felt like I was about to collapse.

Days went by and the doctors were unable to reduce Harry's temperature. He lay motionless in his bed, becoming more delirious with every passing hour. An intravenous line was inserted in his arm to rehydrate his system and deliver strong antibiotics, while ice bags were placed all over his body. I sat next to him, caressing his hand, occasionally venturing outside to the corridor. I sipped on vending machine coffee, called my family and friends, and waited on pins and needles for the doctors' prognosis.

The hospital staff brought in all kinds of equipment, trying everything in their power to reduce Harry's temperature. His sick heart was getting weaker by the minute. I must have looked like a lunatic, as my mind returned over and over to the same question. Would my husband make it? As the seeds of doubt began to outgrow my optimism, a doctor came over, grabbed my hand, and looked into my eyes.

"We re-examined his heart, and have determined that he doesn't have a chance of survival unless we perform surgery immediately. I can assure you that your husband is getting the best treatment and we are doing everything in our power, but without the surgery, he has only a few hours left to live. His heart just won't make it."

"My God, please go do something!" I screamed. "Why are you not operating on him right now?

Why are you not helping him? Why are you still talking to me?"

I didn't want to hear that my husband's life was at risk. All I wanted to hear was that Harry would be fine.

"The operating room is being prepared as we speak. I rescheduled another planned surgery to make room for him, as time is not on his side."

I must have aged at least ten years sitting in that drab green waiting room. The surgery lasted sixteen long hours, during which time Dr. Israel Jacobowitz replaced Harry's aortic valve with an artificial one. As the doctor performed his magic, I counted every dot on the dropped ceiling panels of the waiting room. The bacteria had destroyed not only his original valve, but also the delicate tissue surrounding it.

While sitting beside Harry's lifeless body in the Intensive Care Unit, I began observing the hospital staff as their shifts changed. How I wished that this was only a dream from which I would soon awaken. I dreamed that my dear Israeli would roll down my pajama sleeves and cuddle me for warmth. I would embrace him tightly, breathing in his scent, caressing his scruffy unshaven face. Unfortunately, when I opened my eyes, I was still sitting in the ICU.

Finally the chief surgeon walked in, looking tired. His message was short and clear: "He made it."

"Thank you," I tried to say, but instead, I burst into tears.

"He's still not completely out of the woods," the doctor explained. "He experienced a heart attack during the procedure and it was touch and go for a while. He also suffered extensive muscle damage. I was not only unsure if he would make it, but also whether his body would accept the artificial valve. The only information I can relay is that the surgery was successful and the patient is in stable but critical condition. We'll keep him connected to an artificial heart lung machine until his condition stabilizes and he'll be monitored around the clock."

"The main thing is that he is alive," I repeated over and over. "He is strong, I know him. I trust him.

He will pull through this," I said, filled with hope.

"Mrs. Fisher, one thing I can guarantee is that there are no guarantees as far as outcomes. I have already learned there are no miracles in medicine," Dr. Jacobowitz said kindly.

"Is there something you're not telling me?" I asked.

"Mrs. Fisher, believe me. I would like to tell you that a successful surgery would assure our ultimate victory. However, this is not always the case. It depends on how his heart will respond to this traumatic event."

"He will overcome it. I can vouch for that," I said.

"Let's hope he will. At this moment, all we have is hope."

"I'll stay with him," I said, as I returned to Harry's side and cradled his hand in mine.

The doctor addressed me by my first name and smiled a bit. "Sophia, you need your rest too."

"No," I said. "All I need to do is take care of Harry."

"I understand," he said, as he'd probably said to so many others before me.

Harry's weak failing heart had been kept alive, supported by various devices and defibrillators within arm's reach. That was how he looked: he had tubes protruding from every visible part of his body. While he was still under anesthesia, I sat next to him on his bed, listening to the machine that made his heart beat, as well as the ticking sound of his new valve. I prayed silently, begging God to please save my Harry. The whole family gathered at the hospital, comforting each other. We could do nothing but wait and pray.

Shortly after Harry was transferred from the ICU to his private room, he suffered cardiac arrest. He flatlined and instead of its regular beeping, the monitor emitted an unpleasant whistling sound. I raced through the hospital corridors. The staff attempted to bring him back to life, performing CPR and using defibrillators, but nothing worked. Finally they wheeled him back into the same operating room, where he was once again intubated.

After he was officially declared "clinically dead," I completely fell apart. My head was spinning and I had to be put on a stretcher that was originally brought there for Harry's transport. I lay in the hallway, trying to recover my senses, keeping my eyes closed the whole time. All I could see was his lifeless body being frantically worked on once again by his team of doctors.

There in the corridor, I began thinking about our boys, only four and five years old at the time. I tried to ignore the sinking sensation in my stomach and the sick feeling that permeated my entire body. As luck would have it, this happened on the first day of Rosh Hashana and people all over the greater New York area were praying for Harry's survival. In synagogues from Sheepshead Bay to Rockland County, Jews prayed for his *Refua Shlema*, a special Hebrew prayer for recovery.

All those people praying for him seemed to do the trick, because he was once again revived. I took it as a sign that this was not his time to go. I was ready for anything, but not for my husband's funeral. I felt as if God was of the same opinion. Harry still had so much more to do both in his lifetime and with our family. To this day, I still believe that between the doctors, the private nurse I hired to sit at his bedside around the clock, and the prayers – but most of all, the pull of our love – God brought him back to life.

Due to all the medical intervention, the doctors referred to my husband as a "walking time bomb." As a result of his fluctuating cardiac arrhythmia, Harry had a pacemaker installed. But even with the pacemaker, doctors suggested it would not be enough to keep him alive. He was then transferred to Montefiore Hospital in the Bronx, still attached to a heart and lung machine.

At Montefiore, Harry was subjected to several electrophysiological study tests that proved to be quite invasive. The doctors would artificially simulate cardiac arrest, causing his heart to stop beating. Then they would give him an infusion of powerful medications in order to determine which one would be proper to prescribe, should his heart fail again. They administered everything via his neck artery, which they called the gooseneck. But for all of their work, it proved to be in vain. Harry's weak heart did not respond well to any of the medications administered.

Still, his strong will took over once again. He decided not to put his heart through any more torture and with his own words, he said, "Go ahead, find yourself another crazy man!" and discharged himself from the hospital. Once again, Harry was transferred exactly as before, to Mount Sinai in Manhattan, where he would try the next available option: implanting a cardioverter defibrillator in his abdominal cavity.

This defibrillator was a titanium unit the size of a cigarette box, internally attached directly to his heart muscle. In the event that his heart would cease beating, the defibrillator would immediately revive him with a jolt of electricity. Thankfully, the surgery proved successful.

The rest of the world was put on hold. I was jealous of Ganga, who got to spend time with my children while I felt like a permanent fixture in all these hospitals. I would leave the house first thing in the morning, and if I was lucky, I would see them before they went off to bed at night.

Otherwise, I could only kiss them as they slept, unaware of my presence. The following morning, I would once again race to the hospital before they woke up. How I envied the other couples I passed on the way to the hospital, innocently holding hands and enjoying each other's company.

I was eager to educate myself about Harry's condition, and so I read as much as I could. Pretty soon I considered myself an amateur cardiologist. I also had a friend who was a cardiologist, and he lent me his textbook. I would study it on my way to visit Harry, or when he napped in his hospital bed. Time passed, yet without Harry by my side it seemed to stand still or even stop completely.

On Valentine's Day 1990, after he had spent six long months in three different hospitals, I drove Harry back home. He had shrunk so much during his illness that he appeared to be half the size he once was. He told me that he loved me and I told my darling Israeli counter guy that I loved him right back. We didn't really need the words, as we already knew. But under these circumstances, with questions of his longevity hanging over us, we made it a point to verbalize it. We were unsure of what awaited him.

When Harry regained some of his strength, I taught him how to walk and smile again. I also encouraged him to recognize the small victories. In my many searches, I had come across a book called *Diet for a Strong Heart* by Michio Kushi. Kushi was a leader in macrobiotics, and his book had a tremendous impact on me. It made me reassess not only what I was eating, but also how I was preparing it. I attended his lectures, and learned from his wife Aveline how to look at food in a whole new way. Now I saw it more as a source of health and energy. I had researched all kinds of alternative ways to help Harry, and soon I completely revamped and remodeled our kitchen. I radically changed our lifestyle, even sending my children to school with organic lunches and wearing T-shirts that said, "I eat only organic food."

We had been transformed from kosher gourmet eaters to strict vegetarians. I eliminated all canned and artificial foods and decided against installing a microwave, as I knew it was not a healthy way to cook. It could also interfere with Harry's defibrillator and pacemaker. I began buying smaller sized vegetables and fruits, since they were believed to contain a more concentrated source of energy. I chose them according to the proper seasons, color and taste, along with their healing properties. I began slicing my onions only according to their natural energy patterns, never cutting through the middles, so as not to disturb their flow. I no longer prepared oatmeal from rolled oats, opting instead for whole groats. Engines are measured in horsepower, and horses, considered among the strongest animals around, eat groats.

To ensure that he would survive longer and his heart would strengthen, I started serving Harry groats sprinkled with cinnamon, a dash of maple syrup, sliced apples, roasted walnuts, and a dollop of love to make it taste better. I would do anything to improve his condition. From the day Harry came back home, I quit smoking cigarettes for good. We embraced the macrobiotic lifestyle to the fullest. Like my mother, I was developing an obsession with food, although our motivations were quite different.

Slowly but surely, and to the amazement of all the doctors that treated him, Harry was given a new lease on life. This marked the greatest victory of our lives. It seemed paradoxical that the man known far and wide for his own restaurant food was now brown-bagging his meals when he went back to work. Most of the time I prepared a special macrobiotic risotto from organic brown rice, aduki beans and all kinds of root vegetables. The only salt I added came from my tears of joy. As Harry slowly began to regain his strength, he started to drive himself to work again.

CHAPTER TWENTY

ह

After the Fall of the Iron Curtain

Kosice and Israel Revisited, 1990s

W HILE WE WERE STRUGGLING to keep Harry alive, there had
been a dramatic regime change in Czechoslovakia. As a result
of the collapse of the Berlin Wall and The Velvet Revolution
in November 1989, the Communist government had fallen from power.
Every day as I sat in the hospital room, my eyes were glued to the reports
I saw on CNN. I watched in wonder and awe, carefully observing the
throngs of people in the main squares and hoping to recognize a familiar
face in the crowd. In the initial chaos no one knew what to do with this
sudden new-found freedom, which came without an instruction manual.

Then came another phenomenon that was much closer to my heart
than all the rest of the movements going on in Eastern Europe. I am
talking about the renaissance of Judaism in Slovakia, which had by then
officially split from the Czech Republic. The practice of religion was no
longer prohibited and people began openly acknowledging their Jewish
roots.

One day out of the blue, Daniela Kaufman, my old friend from my early
fashion days in New York, contacted me. Bratislava-born and residing in
Toronto, she had married her longtime boyfriend David and they had
adopted an Orthodox Jewish lifestyle. Ernest Lerner, a Slovakian Jew from
Vrbove and a neighbor of theirs in Toronto, had become very involved
with the events in Slovakia and had suggested that they temporarily move
back to Bratislava.

As Lerner began his Slovakian Jewish outreach program, the Kaufmans would become instrumental in reintroducing the community to Jewish rituals, holidays, history, customs, and of course, food. The Kaufmans initially arrived in Bratislava for a trial period, but to their great delight discovered that they liked being there. The Ronald Lauder Foundation covered their living expenses and soon the young couple moved to historic Kozia Street in the former Jewish ghetto. There they organized Shabbat dinners, taught the reawakening Jewish community the meaning of traditional holidays, and helped educate them in the ways of traditional religious life.

While visiting my parents on one of my many cross-Atlantic trips, I visited the Kaufmans in Bratislava. Daniela told me that they were preparing for a bar mitzvah celebration to be held for a group of boys and men who had never had the opportunity. While in the midst of preparing for the ceremony, the Kaufmans were surprised to discover that some of the males had never been circumcised.

"Can you imagine our shock upon hearing this? How can we perform a bar mitzvah for an uncircumcised male?" my friend asked with a look of great concern.

"What did you do about it?"

"First, we explained to them the principle of *Brit Milah*, circumcision for a male, usually when he is eight days old. Then, we were lucky to find a *mohel* from London that is an expert in this field."

"An Englishman?" I asked, surprised.

"Not really. His name is Dr. Rudy Stern, and he was born here in Bratislava but emigrated to England."

"How did you find out about him?"

"He is a concentration camp survivor. We somehow got in touch with him and he gladly accepted our invitation. When he came to Kozia Street he was absolutely amazed and told us that this was the exact same building the Germans had herded him into in 1942, at age fourteen. His desperate father attempted to hide him and all seven of his brothers in the cellar downstairs, but to no avail. The Hlinka's guardists, who patrolled the buildings every two hours, located all the boys, and along with other Jewish residents they were deported to Auschwitz. Only he and his father survived. His father managed to find refuge at the Spanish embassy, while Rudy and his seven brothers were transported to the camp. Rudy was the only one of eight that made it out," Daniela said.

She paused a moment and then continued, "He explained that he was able to survive because of 'The Boxer,' a man who was also from Bratislava, with whom he developed a deep bond. The Boxer got him a job as a kitchen helper and he would secretly sneak him extra boiled potato skins," Daniela said, filling in the gaps in the story.

"After the war, while in London, Rudy had managed to locate his father, finish his medical studies, and become a *mohel*, continuing the family tradition," Daniela said. "Would you like to know what else?"

"I'm not so sure I want to hear, since I have goose bumps already," I said with some trepidation.

"After Dr. Rudy performed the ritual of circumcision on seven males ranging in age from thirteen to 55, we had a huge *simcha*, a party. We also had quite a surprise waiting for Dr. Rudy. By some great stroke of luck we were able to locate The Boxer and bring him here. You should have seen his reaction. He almost fell over, recognizing him after all those years. They hugged each other for the longest time."

"This is a miracle, a true success story," I said, deeply touched.

Returning to the topic of circumcision, Daniela said, "All sorts of men showed up. For example, there was a man born during the war and while in the concentration camp his mother tried to circumcise him, but apparently she didn't do a very good job. Even some tough guys participated; they wanted to do this, but never had the chance."

"Do you feel safe living here now?" I asked my friend.

"We are fine but some others are pushing the boundaries a bit too far," she replied.

"Why? What is going on?"

"There's a very popular rock'n'roll band called "Shalom." They dress in traditional Hasidic garments and some of their fans have been harassed by undercover police. It's almost a fashion statement now to dress in black, wear Stars of David, grow *peyes* and beards, and observe our holidays. It was pandemonium," she said. "We developed a close friendship with lead singer Petr Muk, who sings about Israel. Although he is not a Jew, he would very much like to convert. He attends our Shabbat dinners and celebrates all the holidays with us," she told me.

"I can't believe it. Rocking and Rolling "Shalom" groupies in Hasidic clothing? I see things have changed quite a bit since I left," I added, with a laugh.

"Well, the regime may have changed, but the hate is still here. A skin-head set a girl's hair on fire at one concert, and Petr swore he could smell gas fumes coming from under the stage at another of his performances. The popularity of the group seems to have created a mass frenzy," Daniela said.

"And do his fans want to convert, too?" I asked.

"No, quite the opposite. It's more of a fashion trend, not a way of life. They have no clue about Judaism, yet they flaunt the Star of David, wear black wide-brimmed hats, and grow facial hair."

"My God, what is going on?" I asked, incredulous.

"I wish I knew. Earlier this year I was questioned by a Jewish woman whose son was enrolled in the yeshiva and would walk around town wearing his yarmulke. For his own safety she begged me to talk him out of it. This just reminded me that things haven't really changed all that much. Now we have skinheads instead of Nazis shouting Fascist slogans, and their movement is growing fast," she said.

"Perhaps it will take some time to get better," I said. I felt hopeful but was also skeptical that things could really turn around overnight.

"Maybe one day. But in the meantime there is no end in sight. I worry about Petr. He was diagnosed as bipolar but refuses to undergo any treatment. He still comes for Shabbat dinners and we remain very close. His fans still love and follow him, but I don't know whether all this attention and controversy has become too much for him to bear," Daniela said.

I also became enthusiastic about their mission in Bratislava. My first planned event to raise funds for the Kaufmans mission was a chamber music concert at my home. I invited people from the local community, as well as friends and family members. As they arrived, the guests were welcomed at the door by the dulcet tones of a harpist. I served delicious food and fine wine. Harry embraced the idea with gusto and he had all the food prepared and catered by Jerusalem II.

Seeing him back in his element and playing the ever-charming and warm host we all knew him to be filled me with joy. The proceeds from the event went to the Lauder foundation and I delivered the funds directly to Rabbi Chaskel Besser, who was then the spiritual leader of the cosmetics magnate's foundation. The Lauder Foundation doubled the amount and the money was sent to Bratislava. I became an active member of the International Committee and was eager to continue with this work.

"Daniela, take good care of yourself and your family. You and David are doing a great mitzvah, and I want to let you know that I am currently working on another fundraising event for you in New York. My friend

Vicki, a Jewish woman from Piestany who had emigrated with her sister back in 1969, supplied me with a long list of names and addresses of resettled Czechoslovakian Jews in the tri-state area. I am already hard at work on this next event. I invited the chairman of the World Jewish Congress to welcome the guests and the music will be provided by the famous Rabbi Shlomo Carlebach himself."

"We really need and appreciate all the support we can get. Sophia, how can I thank you?" Daniela asked, her voice filled with emotion.

"No thanks are necessary. You do your mitzvahs and I will do mine," I said, before wishing her a warm farewell.

The Kaufmans left Bratislava for Israel but remained in close touch with Petr Muk. He went to visit them a few times, but he wasn't doing well and even attempted suicide. His divorce soon followed, and after finally undergoing psychiatric treatments, it seemed as though he had gotten his life back under control. He remarried and was by all appearances living a happy life until his tragic death in May 2010. A lethal combination of antidepressants and alcohol had ended his life.

After a bomb attack near Daniela's house in Israel nearly killed her son, she and her family packed up again and moved back to Toronto. Meanwhile, I continued to follow the news from Slovakia regarding the rebirth of our nation. What had seemed impossible a few years ago had now become a reality. But my most important task was still taking care of my Harry and overseeing his health. I would do anything to keep him alive, and by now, fear had become my constant companion.

Life's unexpected challenges can come without warning at any given moment. Only eighteen months after it was first implanted, Harry's body began to reject his defibrillator. It protruded through his abdominal cavity and we feared another infection, which would gravely affect his already weakened heart and new valve. The doctors considered inserting a new unit into the other side of his abdominal cavity.

I had a very hard time accepting the news and I sought out new opinions. After a great deal of research, I discovered that a skilled team of doctors in Houston was using a new generation of smaller defibrillators that were the size of a matchbox. Deciding it was worth the risk, I flew with Harry to Texas the next day and he was admitted to the hospital on the spot.

After an elaborate series of tests and exams, the lead doctor and his team presented us with an unexpected option. He assured us that Harry's heart was strong enough by now and that he no longer required the de-fibrillator. They removed it leaving only the wires, with the pads attached directly to the heart muscle. The pads were left intact in order to avoid further open heart surgery.

Suddenly life appeared bright and promising, and I came to my own conclusion: my groats had worked! Harry and I began enjoying our life once again, and together we reveled in raising our two sons. What's more, we fulfilled the promise we had made to one another so long ago – both boys had their Bar Mitzvahs in Israel. As Harry led our sons to the West-ern Wall and they read their Torah portions, he was brimming with pride. He also taught them how to wear *tefillin*, the two little boxes with black leather straps that Jewish men wrap around their arm and their head in a centuries-old prayer ritual. I felt satisfied knowing that my husband cared so much for his children.

After we returned to New York we had another celebration for those who could not make the trip to Israel. Harry was still holding on, but he seemed to be growing weaker and weaker right before my eyes.

On many nights I would lie awake just to listen for the beats that reas-sured me he was still alive. I often visited him at work just to check on his condition, and I began to get used to seeing an ambulance parked right in front of Jerusalem II.

Outwardly I had mastered the art of appearing stoic, but inside I was crumbling. All those days and nights sitting in the emergency rooms of various New York hospitals had simply exhausted me, both emotionally and physically. Waiting and not knowing my husband's fate was literally unbearable. To keep busy and distract myself from the grim reality of what was going on, I would rearrange the furniture in the waiting rooms.

Despite the medications, Harry's heart condition continued to worsen. He got winded more easily than ever, and at times he would have to stop to catch his breath while walking from his car to the front door of our house. As these episodes became more and more frequent, I sought spiri-tual guidance from highly respected rabbis and adhered to all the advice I was given. One rabbi gave me the most uplifting advice of all. He told me that when God gave the camel its hump, he made sure it would be able to bear its burdens.

"So, is your Harry getting better?" Timka asked one afternoon, during one of our regular phone conversations.

My dear friend Timka had always been my most steadfast supporter.

After earning a Master's Degree in economics, and eventually divorcing her unfaithful husband, Timka was now raising her firstborn son in Banska Bystrica. As always, she managed to take care of everything herself, and it appeared that no obstacle was too big for her to overcome. She was the same Timka, forever smiling, filled with ironic humor and boundless energy. But it was only a facade.

"I can't seem to shake off the fear," I told Timka. "But I'm still praying for the best, and doing whatever is within my power to help my husband."

"Sophia, you must stay strong in your faith. Believe me, he will be fine," she tried to reassure me.

"From your mouth to God's ears."

"Let's make a promise to each other," Timka said.

"What kind of promise?" I asked.

"When your Harry and I get better, can we go to Rome together, all three of us? I would love to sit on the famous Spanish Steps, sip an espresso, eat gelato and soak up some warm Italian rays of sun," Timka said, almost dreamlike.

"What are you getting at, Timka? I'm not sure I understand."

"Remember when I told you about the pain I had been experiencing in my lower abdomen?" she asked.

"Are you trying to tell me you're pregnant?" I joked.

"I wish. Unfortunately, something other than a baby is growing inside me."

My heart began to thump, as I knew in my gut that what she was about to tell me would not be good news. "Please, no more beating around the bush. Tell me what it is I need to know," I demanded.

"I have cervical cancer."

For the next few moments it felt as if time had screeched to a halt. Her words fell on me like boulders from the sky. I was so stunned that it took me quite some time before I could speak again.

"Tell me this isn't true. What have your doctors told you?"

"They say that it's curable, and since I'm not yet forty, my prognosis is excellent."

"Timka, have no worries. Before you know it, you will be sitting on those Spanish Steps in Rome with Harry and me," I vowed to my dear old friend.

"I'm already looking forward to it," she said. "And hopefully by then I won't be wearing a wig."

I detected neither sorrow nor fear in her voice, but knowing her as well as I did, I knew that she was worried. I introduced her to macrobiotics and explained how it had helped Harry and so many other people I'd met in my classes. She listened intently to everything I told her and was eager to begin immediately.

"Sophia, hypothetically speaking, should the worst occur, would you take care of my affairs?"

"If necessary, I would take care of anything for you. But since I know you will beat this, let's not talk about it anymore and focus instead on our plans for Rome."

"I knew I could count on you," she said. "To Rome!"

To say that Timka's ordeal was heart-wrenching is an understatement. But after undergoing intensive treatments she emerged healthy and cancer-free. She made a full recovery and soon met a new, much younger boyfriend. They wanted to have a child, but with her history of cervical cancer they both knew that their chances were slim. However, miracles do happen every once in a while. Timka married her young groom Igor, and together they became the proud and joyous parents of a little boy named Igorko.

My two adolescent sons and I attended their wedding in Slovakia. Timka looked radiant and was glowing from within, but I was not. While the cancer showed mercy to Timka, my father was not so lucky. He began to deteriorate right in front of me, another victim of this ravaging disease. My father had lived a long life and my hope for him, as well as any elderly person, would be that death would arrive compassionately in his sleep, without suffering. I stayed in the hospital with my sick father in Kosice, sitting next to him for hours on end. I had an open-ended ticket and at one point I had to return home because of the children and Harry.

I had made my return reservation, but just as I arrived at the airport the flights from Kosice were canceled because of fog. On the way to Poprad, Slovakia, via bus for a two-hour drive to the nearest airport, I contemplated whether the fog was a sign that I should have stayed at my father's bedside. But it was too late. The plane ticket couldn't be exchanged. When I arrived back home to Brooklyn, I was met with the awful news that my father had passed away the night before.

I flew back to Kosice right away, carrying the same luggage I hadn't even had time to unpack. Mely, Hanka, and I spoke very little, as there was not much to be said. I was jet-lagged and emotionally drained.

After we each said our final farewells to the man we loved so much, we buried our father, Yaakov Manisevic, in the Jewish Cemetery in Kosice on November 28, 1998.

⅍

CHAPTER TWENTY-ONE

The Saddest Chapter of My Life

New York and Texas, 1999–2000

A S TIME PASSED, Harry's heart became weaker and the visits to the hospital became more frequent. I decided to become even more proactive in searching for new treatments, doctors and courses of action that would prolong Harry's life and perhaps even improve its quality. On November 15, 1999, our nineteenth wedding anniversary, we flew to Texas once again to see if he was a viable candidate for a heart transplant.

Doctors informed us that in order for him to be put on the waiting list, which could take years, we would have to relocate to Texas. They also explained that he would have to be close to the hospital. A complication could strike at a moment's notice, or a heart could become available and he would have to be ready for immediate surgery. New York was just too far away, so we opted to go back home to be put on the waiting list at Columbia Presbyterian Hospital, which has one of the finest heart transplant programs in the world.

Before long yet another complication arose. The prongs from the wires that had been left behind in Harry's abdominal cavity began to protrude through his skin. As his condition worsened we feared that he would suffer another major infection. He was put on the waiting list for a heart, but because of the deterioration, he was not considered a viable candidate. According to the experts, the heart transplant was simply out of the question. He would never survive it.

We consulted with Dr. Mehmet Oz, who sat with us for over an hour, exploring every possible option. Finally, after speaking with Dr. Craig

Smith, a cardiothoracic surgeon, we decided that Harry would undergo two surgeries that had the potential to improve his condition.

The first surgery would be to remove the prongs and wires in his abdomen, left behind from his implanted defibrillator. The second surgery would be to remove the electrodes with the pads that were still attached to his heart muscle. Finally, a bypass would be performed.

Because his enlarged heart could no longer pump enough oxygen through his body, Harry was becoming cyanotic. Edema had set in, his legs so swollen, he could barely stand and he was bleeding from the wound caused by the protrusion of the prongs. The large, open wound in his stomach took six weeks to heal.

The first surgery was scheduled for December 31, 1999, the end of one century and the beginning of another. The day before the first day of the new millennium, while people worldwide celebrated, a team of surgeons removed the prongs and wires that were causing the internal and external abdominal bleeding. At the stroke of midnight, standing alone next to his bed and watching multicolored fireworks explode over the New York City skyline, I could not even shed a tear. I prayed and hoped for the best. I loved my husband and wanted so desperately for him to recover.

The second surgery was scheduled for Tuesday, February 15, 2000, the first thing in the morning. Tuesday is supposed to be a lucky day for Jews, so I hoped that some of that luck might rub off on my dear husband. Dr. Craig Smith and his accomplished team of surgeons were to remove the leftover electrodes and pads from the Cardioverter Defibrillator that were still attached to Harry's heart muscle. But when they opened Harry up, the doctors discovered that after being in place for more than eight years the electrode attachments had calcified and created numerous layers, binding Harry's heart muscles. These layers literally formed a cast around his heart. In order to reach the muscle itself, the surgeons had to chisel away at it as if it were a suit of armor. As it turned out, the main reason that Harry's heart couldn't function properly was that this once-yielding material had now become its biggest restriction.

As Harry was being rolled away on the stretcher, we held hands. He pressed my palm into his and said, "I love you." And with those words he left this world for eternity. In life, some people leave their mark of distinction in unique ways. They meet every challenge head-on, facing down obstacles with unmitigated resolve and determination. That was my Harry.

On February 17, 2000, we buried Harry Fisher beside his father at Beth Abraham Cemetery in East Brunswick, New Jersey. As was the custom, we sat *shiva* for the whole week. I transformed our house into a small temple, its door open to all. Even though it was my own home, it nevertheless felt like a foreign place.

Every day crowds of people would gather to pray, eat, and remember my husband. I knew that I would be unable to deal with the grief and loneliness by myself. Some people prefer to be left alone while mourning, but not I. It was a great comfort to be in the company of so many others who also loved Harry.

According to the Torah, only the closest relatives of the deceased sit *shiva*, the Jewish ritual of mourning. The mirrors are covered, and the family abstains from washing, showering, cooking and working. For an entire week we sit on wooden boxes, without shoes, and with our shirts ripped, in order to express how torn we feel inside. Sitting there in my bare feet, everything felt so surreal, as if a part of me had died along with Harry.

When the *shiva* period concluded, my boys and I could no longer avoid our merciless reality.

Mechanically, I ventured outside to the backyard, into the foggy cold February day and walked around the block holding my sons' hands, as was the tradition. In this symbolic way, we accompanied Harry's soul on its journey to eternal rest. My days were now filled with an emptiness that enveloped my soul, entered my heart, and never left my side. Without Harry, life had lost all meaning.

For the entire year following Harry's death, our sons Henry and David, then fourteen and fifteen years old, recited the *Kaddish*, the Jewish memorial prayer, three times a day. They never missed a single day. As my dear Israeli up in heaven heard these two fine young men reciting the Mourners' *Kaddish* through the mists, he must certainly have been smiling that huge bright smile of his. Thankfully, his death was not in vain. Because of Harry's case, a new generation of Cardioverter Defibrillators was developed. The new models no longer require pads that attach directly to the heart, but rather to electrodes. As a result of my husband's sacrifice, thousands of lives have been saved.

After Harry's passing, when time had closed the open wounds a bit, I learned how to be thankful for those ten years we were gifted with after his first surgery. At that time the doctors were counting how many hours he had left to live, but instead of hours, we were given ten more wonderful years. Although sad, I was still relieved that the boys had gotten the chance to know their father, even if it wasn't for long enough.

Harry and I continued loving each other from one Valentine's Day in 1990 until another Valentine's Day in 2000 when he said "I love you" for the last time.

For more than half a year I moved around as if in a fog. Suddenly the house had become too big, and the world too dark. I could not accept the fact I had become a widow; that I would never again see my husband, feel his warmth, or smell his scent. I disagree with those who say that you can prepare yourself for the loss of a loved one. How does one get used to it? His departure completely paralyzed our lives. Harry departed just at the moment his sons needed him the most. Who would become their role model now? How would I raise two young men on my own?

I went through my husband's belongings, putting aside his perfectly ironed shirts and pants, before placing them right back on the shelves. I couldn't part with them. I attempted to continue living as we had before but I was finding it impossible. From time to time I was so filled with despair that I couldn't get myself to leave the house. I felt that when Harry died, so did my identity. Without him, I was no longer sure who I was in my beloved America.

CHAPTER TWENTY-TWO

ৰ্চ

Moving On

New York, Slovakia, 2000

T HE BOYS WERE ALREADY in high school at the Yeshiva of Flatbush
and they were becoming more independent. After their father's
death, they grew up rather fast. I felt that their needs were changing and I played less of a role in their lives. I felt as if nobody needed me;
there was no one waiting for me at the house. There were only cold walls,
as well as objects that had turned into artifacts, losing all their sentimental
value. Everything reminded me of Harry. My friends in Slovakia and Italy
had their own lives with their own worries and joys. I remained alone and
felt as if I didn't belong anywhere.

My partnership with Broadway's Jerusalem II and Mr. Broadway ended
with Harry's passing.

Because of an influx of new kosher restaurants popping up all over
Manhattan, our glory days were coming to an end. After someone else
had broken my brother-in-law Teddy's record from the Guinness Book
of World Records, he became obsessed with reclaiming it. Without delay,
Teddy and his "flying pizza pie" embarked on a delivery to the southern-
most tip of Australia, the farthest geographical distance from New York
City.

Once again, with a yarmulke on his head and a smile on his face, Teddy
traveled by plane and train. He got lost a few times but still managed
to deliver his by now $8,000 dollar pizza pie to the right location. He
was able to do it in eight days, without missing a Shabbat or violating
any Jewish laws. Once again, he made it back into the Guinness Book of

World Records, claiming that until the day comes when someone delivers pizza to the moon, his name will remain in that book forever.

One year after Harry's death, Teddy sold Jerusalem II to new owners and later sold his shares in Mr. Broadway as well. Even now, whenever I find myself in the neighborhood, I still stop in to check on things and have an occasional meal with friends.

I was learning that the wheel of life is always turning, sometimes carrying us to our destiny, at other times crushing us beneath its weight. How did I feel? Miserable, though I didn't intend to stay that way forever. I realized that lonely people become bitter. Pain toughens you up, while suffering does nothing but age you. I didn't want to become cynical and angry. I knew that I had to get up on my feet again.

Taking Henry and David to school had become the only reason for me to wake up in the morning. One morning after I dropped them off, I aimlessly drove up and down the streets of Brooklyn. As I looked around, I felt that I had lost not only my identity, but also my sense of belonging. I was beginning to understand that although I felt lost, life still continued on, relatively unchanged beyond the tragedy and sorrow I was experiencing.

My moods would fluctuate rapidly from anger to agitation to sadness, and even to jealousy. I was still a young vibrant woman, and I chose not to dwell on what fate had in store for me. I couldn't live just for my memories. I tried to resurrect that old Sophia who had fallen asleep inside of me. I never gave up before so why should I now? After all, Henry and David were still here and I needed to make plans to rejoin life.

Luckily I didn't have to, because my good friends in the neighborhood had already made plans for me. They arranged a girls' spa retreat at the New Age Health Spa in upstate New York, near Lake Neversink. Four of us went there by car and participated in all kinds of activities, including climbing a five- story high makeshift wooden tower while strapped into a harness. We went through a brief training session and, of course, I was the first to volunteer to make the climb. From the ground, all of my friends were cheering me on as I slowly scaled to the top of the tower. Standing breathless at the summit, totally exhilarated, I felt as if I had conquered Mt. Everest. In my moment of triumph, it never occurred to me that I would somehow have to get down from my peak.

The instructor shouted at me to jump, since that was the only way down. Everyone assured me that I was safe in my harness. All I heard was that I had to free fall into nothing and trust that everything they said was true. I held my breath for a second and said, "God, I'm all yours," then took the plunge. After conquering this challenge, the fear of moving on with my life slowly dissipated. Once again time proved to be the best healer, acting as a salve for my wounds. But I also needed a distraction of some kind or another.

I didn't know what I was seeking, but I knew something was missing.

One day as I was parking my car in the driveway, I noticed the silhouette of a woman sitting on the bench in my backyard. I could only see her from the back. Upon hearing the sound of the gate closing behind me, she turned to face me.

"Vicky?" I almost screamed in shock.

"Sophia, how are you?" she said.

I was utterly caught off guard. "What are you doing here?" I asked.

"Do I need an invitation to come visit my friend?"

"Of course, you can visit anytime. It's just that I wasn't expecting you. What a nice surprise! Come, let's go inside," I said.

"Sophia, I worry about you. Just take a look at yourself. You are avoiding everybody. I understand how you feel and what you had to endure, but don't forget you still have your two sons. They need you now more than ever. I know you will find the strength to see this through," Vicky said.

I hadn't seen her since the funeral and the *shiva*. I always enjoyed her company and her unwavering good mood, which I found infectious.

"I thank God every day that I have them," I said. "But contrary to what you think, I am not avoiding anybody. That's just how you see it. Besides, I am very involved with the boys' activities," I answered, looking at her through dark sunglasses.

"I am sure they are a great comfort to you," she said kindly.

"Well . . ." here I stopped, exploding into tears.

Vicky took my convulsing body into her arms, trying to calm me down without much success. Once I regained my composure, she guided me to her car and drove me to a nearby coffee shop. As we settled into our seats, Vicky looked me straight in the eye and said, "Listen to me and listen to me well. There will be no more sitting at home feeling sorry for yourself. Harry's end does not mean it is your end, too. I am aware that it hurts, probably even more than I can imagine. I know you're feeling lost and confused, but all of this will pass," she reassured me.

We ordered two cappuccinos and two almond croissants.

"I resent being an object of pity," I said. "I am so lost without Harry, and I am not used to being alone." I started to sob again. "My mother used to say, 'When people envy you, it is fine, but when they feel sorry for you, you ought to do something about it.'"

"Sophia, it looks like you need a change of scenery to clear your head. Maybe you would consider taking a short vacation?" Vicky asked timidly.

"What do you mean? All by myself?"

"No, that's not what I meant at all."

"I'm sorry for snapping," I said, feeling a bit awkward about my outburst.

"We can go somewhere together. You just lost ten years of your life because you always had to be near the hospital. Now you need to step back out of your shell. I think a small trip would do you some good. Don't be so hard on yourself. Who can handle loneliness? There is no training for being a young widow.

Give yourself a break."

"But everybody knows me as Mrs. Fisher, Harry's widow. This upsets me a bit, too, because it's a constant reminder. I know that tragedy tends to bring people together and that the most beautiful things in the world are our rewards for suffering, but sometimes I wish I could just disappear. Sometimes I wish I could become anonymous and get lost in the real genuine New York," I told her.

"But you have to start making some real, tangible plans," she said.

"David has already made some, but I feel very uncomfortable about it all. Maybe you can help me make up my mind. He showed me some information he got on a summer camp in Australia and New Zealand. It will be a six-week skiing trip, with a stopover in Hawaii for some beach time," I said. "They both want to go."

"Oh, how exciting. That sounds perfect. What's your problem with it?" she asked, her brow furrowed.

"Vicky, I've never been apart from them for so long. You're talking about halfway around the world and they're still so young," I argued.

"Sophia, what are you talking about? Henry will be sixteen, and David, fifteen. They aren't babies anymore," Vicky said, trying her hardest to persuade me.

"Yes, I know, but still. Call me selfish, but I don't think I'm ready yet. I didn't take David seriously when he first told me, so I haven't had time to even consider it. I don't think I'm ready to have them away from me for an entire summer. They have never been to a sleepaway camp before, only day camp, and I worry about them considering all they've been through. I don't know how I can go a full six weeks without them. I would miss them so," I said, defending my stance.

"I think this will be a great opportunity for all three of you, and you will have the whole summer to sort things out before you reach a decision. Just give it some thought, that's all I'm asking. Think of it as a new beginning," she said.

I felt a sharp pain in my heart. I was overprotective of my sons, mainly because I had missed spending so much time with them while nursing Harry through his illness. "I promise to think about it," I said. "But I'm not guaranteeing anything."

Vicky drove me back home and we continued our conversation, but this time, the subject turned to Harry. Laughing and crying in the kitchen, we shared our memories. Vicky insisted that I go with her to Broadway shows, movies, lunches, concerts, parties, or even just for a cup of coffee or a glass of wine – anything to get me out of the house. My friend had my best interests at heart and I knew that she was right.

Before long my calendar was filled with invitations to Shabbat dinners and holiday celebrations with family, friends, and neighbors. My sons and I took great comfort in the sense of community these events provided. Everyone showed us kindness and compassion, and once again we felt a true sense of belonging.

The same day that Vicky dropped by, my sons tried to convince me that going to the camp, Kanfei Nesharim, was a great idea. They would benefit from being there, they argued, and besides, they would be accompanied by a rabbi from New York University who was an avid skier. There was also the fact that they would travel as a group. "What could possibly go wrong?" David asked in his most convincing tone.

While Harry was still alive, the boys had never gone to sleepaway camp like most of their friends. As if he knew something long before I did, Harry always wanted to have his family near him. I remembered many occasions when the boys would come crying to me, wishing they too could go to sleepaway camp.

But they understood their father's devotion and didn't argue. I felt such guilt. Their father's sickness had impacted their childhood in ways they couldn't even begin to comprehend.

Harry never had the chance to play basketball or baseball with his sons, but he cheered them on from the sidelines. He never went skiing on the slopes, but he was always the first to greet them at the bottom of the hill. He was an ever-present father in their daily lives, driving them to school every morning, and he was always there for them, whenever they needed him.

"Mom, are you listening?" Henry asked, unable to restrain himself any longer. He was truly my son.

When they were distributing patience, he was standing at the end of the line, just as I was.

"Do you know what, my dear?" I said, pausing for dramatic effect.

"Does this mean you are going to let us go?" David asked.

"Yes, you can go with my blessings."

"Mom, I can't tell you how excited we are. This will be awesome!" he shouted.

"Yes, I believe we all need this. Let's pack. Hawaii, Australia, and New Zealand, here you come!" I exclaimed.

Summer arrived, and soon the boys embarked upon their adventure. Accompanied by my sisters, Melanie and Hanka, who were there for support, I watched my sons leave on their own for the very first time. Their aunts kissed them and wished them safe travels as I waved goodbye.

Returning home, I never felt more alone. Without a second thought, I reserved a flight back to Kosice so that I could spend some time with my mother. I quickly packed my luggage, without any gifts or concrete plans. I was escaping again, this time from the house where everywhere I turned, I ran into Harry. I was also making my way to the Spanish Steps in Rome with Timka, so at least the two of us could enjoy a good cup of coffee. I wanted to help make her dream come true.

Just being with my mother gave me so much comfort that I could immediately feel my mood lightening. Here, in the place where I had grown up, I was not constantly confronted with memories of my husband.

A week later Timka picked me up at my mother's house and we drove off to Rome.

"Sophia, how are you coping?" my friend asked.

"There are no words to describe how I feel. What have I done wrong to deserve this?"

"I have no answers, but I continue searching. You must hold tight to your faith that everything will turn out fine."

"Let's just head to the Spanish Steps and have that espresso you've dreamed about for so long," I said, as I slipped my arm through hers. It seemed that the older Timka got, the more beautiful she became, both inside and out.

"Timka, since I don't drive a stick shift, you are the designated driver. I'll be your navigator," I said.

"Fantastic."

"I'll call Ambretta and let her know we'll be arriving in a few days."

This was our "Easy Rider" trip in a rental car, since Timka's car had no air conditioning. Traveling through Tuscany, we enjoyed the magnificent landscape and stopped along the way for the occasional panini or cup of espresso. We slept in hotels without even making reservations, sitting up in bed together like schoolgirls. We caught up on all the gossip and ordered scrumptious meals, both in the restaurant and in our room.

When we finally made it to the Spanish Steps, Timka sat down wearily. I tried to steer the conversation away from Harry and toward her and her life. Deep in my gut, I felt that there was something she wasn't telling me. Suddenly I realized that she hadn't mentioned anything about her second husband.

"Why haven't you mentioned Igor at all?" I asked my friend. "Is everything all right between the two of you?"

In a matter-of-fact voice, Timka told me that she didn't want to discuss any painful subjects. Her second marriage hadn't worked out, but since we were two girls on vacation, there would be no complaining.

"Why didn't you tell me?" I asked. "I am ashamed," she confessed. "Why?"

"Because it's a terrible situation. I don't want to burden you with it," Timka said.

"Are you serious? We're friends through good and bad. There is no reason to keep anything from me."

"Did you expect me to bring my problems here to Rome? No way, I am not going to spoil this experience for either of us. Sophia, you know I am not a complainer."

"Come on, you expect me to talk about everything over the phone, yet you couldn't tell me that your second marriage was in trouble?"

"Nobody knows it yet. I feel miserable. I only wish I could have a good cry," she said.

"So why don't you?" I asked. "You are the one that was always there for me, not the other way around."

"I don't want to appear weak. I actually think I've forgotten how to."

"Crying helps a lot more than you can even imagine. Do you know what? I will teach you how to cry again. Our next trip together will be to Israel. We will visit all the holy sites and I'm sure that at the Western Wall you will be unable to hold back the river of salty tears," I said.

"How ironic that I have to travel halfway around the world so I can relearn how to cry," she said, laughing.

"Life is a perpetual search and I've found that for every answer I receive, three more questions pop up in its place. What's more, we will be together again. But for now, let's go visit Ambretta and her family."

Ambretta spoiled us big time, even serving us breakfast in bed. She invited all of her family and friends over and we sat around until the wee hours of the morning, reminiscing and feasting on the Italian sweets she had prepared especially for our visit. Her kind face hadn't changed and I felt peaceful and at ease.

Before we continued on, Timka and I spent an entire day at the beach, soaking up the sun. Finally we bid our farewells to Ambretta and her family and made our way to Milan, the fashion capital of Italy. On a Friday afternoon at the Galleria in the Piazza del Duomo, I noticed a Lubavitcher Jew. I tentatively approached and asked him where the nearest synagogue was, as I was preparing to observe Shabbat that evening.

As it turned out, he was the son-in-law of the Chief Rabbi of Milan, and he insisted that Timka and I join him at his family's home for Shabbat dinner. We accepted his kind invitation and enjoyed ourselves at the lavish table. His family and I began to speak about New York, and when I mentioned who my late husband was, they told me they had been devoted customers of Jerusalem II. They remembered Harry as a kind, gentle and caring man and held him in high regard. As it turned out, my husband had done many more generous deeds for people than I ever knew. He was never one to brag about his devotion to helping others, and he kept it to himself.

I broke off a piece of beautiful golden challah bread and thanked God for everything that had been given to me. In my prayers, I expressed my gratitude for the gift of love, the gift of freedom, the gift of friendship, the gift of motherhood, and the gift of being Jewish. Now it was my turn to give back and fulfill the promises I had made. As it is in life, whenever one door slams shut, another one opens. I was ready to walk through.

Upon my return to America, I promised myself that I would actively participate in the game of life and learn to live again. The trip to Italy had renewed my spirit and opened up the shell I had crawled into. Back in Brooklyn, I happily returned to my community and synagogue and soon became more active in my boys' academic lives.

Along with my friend Frieda, I also enrolled in the Institute of Integrated Nutrition, where we studied alternative health and healing modalities. We earned our degrees as Holistic Health Counselors, accredited by the American Association of Drugless Practitioners, and I soon began to consult, lecture, and write. For more than two years, the *Jewish Press* published my articles on food and healing in a column called, "21st Century Nutrition." Through workshops and seminars we organized at our homes, Frieda and I shared our knowledge of nutrition and healthy living. We demonstrated healthful cooking techniques, and held yoga and Pilates classes. We called it "The Women's Circle."

My friend Vicky was my partner in cultural activities. One evening after a concert at Lincoln Center, we went for a quick bite at Josephina's, a restaurant across the street. Out of nowhere, I heard a soothing familiar voice coming from the table behind us.

"Sophia?"

As I turned around, there he was, Sofio.

"Is it really you, Bella?" he asked excitedly.

"Yes, it's me. What are you doing here?" I answered in utter shock.

"I come here quite often. I live right around the corner."

"Really? I can't believe that after twenty years I'm seeing you again."

Vicky was well aware of our past and she soon politely excused herself and went home. Sofio joined me at my table. While sipping Italian wine, we filled each other in on the events of the last twenty years and reminisced about the good old days. It felt so good to be in his company again. Here we were, twenty years older, each of us having lived full lives, with our feet firmly planted on the ground. Being around Sofio again felt as comfortable as an old pair of fuzzy slippers and I could feel that old flame beginning to rekindle.

Being with Sofio again was exactly what the doctor ordered. To feel desirable again as a woman, not just as a mother, a widow, or a housekeeper, was fantastic. The old Sophia had been reawakened. I wanted someone to spend time with and talk to, and I had a sudden urge to love and be loved again.

Even though Sofio and I had a strong attraction and enjoyed each other's company immensely, it was not in the stars. He loved my children very much, but I didn't want to deprive him of the experience of having his own child with a younger woman. I knew that not even one hundred Gypsy palm readers would find another baby in my future. We parted amicably and three years later he eventually settled down. As he turned fifty years old, he did marry a younger woman and he now has two beautiful little daughters.

I began to feel as though I was spending more time in the air than on the ground. My mother became ill with dementia and she was no longer herself. In the beginning it didn't seem serious, but even so, I wished she would come home with me so that I could take care of her. I had plenty of space in my half-empty house, and a room that she would find comfortable. At first she started to forget places, then people, and as the disease progressed, she began wandering off and getting lost. I took her to the doctor in Kosice and his exam confirmed our worst fears. He said that Mother was suffering from Alzheimer's disease.

In the beginning she would just shuffle around with no sense of direction. She would enter a room only to forget why she had gone there in the first place. When outside, she would turn in the wrong direction, heading toward a neighbor's house, and would become confused and agitated. Later on, she began to have trouble dressing herself, and would constantly refer to people from the past. The disease was stealing her away from us right before our eyes. She refused to come to America with me, claiming she felt safer in her own apartment.

My sisters, their children, and I took turns visiting Mother, and we arranged for around- the-clock care. It was difficult for us to witness this strong survivor of a woman fading away so quickly. How horrible to see your own parent as a child, needing constant attention. Soon, our own mother no longer recognized us. There was nothing left for us to do.

In the spring of 2002 the time finally came for me to fulfill the promise I had made at my grandfather Chaim's grave all those years ago. I was determined to begin renovating the Jewish cemetery in Porubka. I hired a crew of workers who used bulldozers to clear out the overgrowth and raze the old trees. They set proper boundaries around the cemetery and restored it to its once pristine condition. It took one week to uncover 56 abandoned, eroded, decimated gravestones. The workers brought in gravel, exposed the path, and installed a rustic fence with a wooden gate adorned with a large Star of David.

Timka was my manager by proxy, and it pleased me so that my mother was able to visit the cemetery with me. I knew how proud she was. When all the work had been completed, I hired my former neighbor in Porbuka, Josef Kudlac, to maintain the cemetery to my standards. He kept his word, and to this day he is still managing it.

Over a period of five years, Mother's condition continued to worsen. It was as if she had become a child again. We took care of her as best we could, but we lost her long before she physically passed away in December 2006. We three sisters had now become true orphans. Standing at her grave with Kosice blanketed in snow, we mourned and grieved the loss of our dear mother. We sat silently, said our goodbyes, and thanked her for everything she had done for us. It was the last time we ever saw that Auschwitz number tattooed on her arm: A-9103. Simone Leah Manisevicova was finally at peace. For the whole week, we sat Shiva in her apartment on Czechoslovakian Army Street.

In the old synagogue on Pushkinova Street in Kosice, my sisters and I dedicated a stained glass window in memory of our parents. It was the same synagogue where, as young girls, we had checked out the boys from the balcony. I am still hoping that eventually one of the synagogue windows will be dedicated to artist Ludovit Feld. As his Holocaust drawings aren't appropriate to hang on the walls of my home, they are safely stored away. But perhaps one day, as Harry had wished so long ago in Kosice, Feld's masterpieces will one day be exhibited in a museum for the world to see.

Shortly after Mother's funeral, I returned home to Brooklyn. Even though I was born in Czechoslovakia, I no longer felt I belonged there. America was now my home. But I still couldn't bear to part with my parents' apartment in the Kosice of my past. To this day, I still own it.

In May 2005, Vicky and I decided to join the first worldwide reunion of the wave of Jewish emigrants who left Slovakia, part of the former Czechoslovakia, beginning in 1968. In the stately Hotel Carlton in Bratislava, we joined the gathering, which brought together more than three hundred Jews from all over the world. As name-tagged people began to recognize each other, I could feel the excitement building in the air. With every embrace, it was as if the forty-year separation had melted away. Here we were – dissidents, unwanted enemies of the state, even refugees – being welcomed by the Slovakian Minister of Foreign Affairs. Every year since then, we have continued this tradition, leaving our homes in disparate parts of the world to reunite in Slovakia, or even in Israel.

While in Bratislava I took advantage of the opportunity to visit the memorial of the famous Rabbi Chatam Sofer (1762-1839). Rabbi Sofer was the son of a long line of rabbis, and by age thirteen he was already lecturing. At that time, reforms in Judaism were taking hold across Europe, and Rabbi Sofer became their most vocal opponent. To this day, many Orthodox families still follow his teachings, and yeshivas and synagogues throughout the world are named in his honor. But a curious mystery surrounds his final resting place.

Rabbi Sofer was buried beneath the Bratislava Castle, along the banks of the Danube River. But in 1943, the cemetery was destroyed to make room for new roads. Years later, it was discovered that somehow the graves of Rabbi Sofer and 22 of his loyal devotees had remained untouched. When Slovakia gained its independence in 1992, the roads were moved and the gravesites were restored. On July 8, 2002, a mausoleum was erected in Rabbi Sofer's honor. For Orthodox Jews all over the world, it is now a well-known tourist attraction.

When I visited the site, I was pleased to see how beautifully and respectfully it had been redeveloped. In 1990, the first time I visited, I had to descend a ladder into a manhole leading to a tunnel, just to reach his gravesite. According to tradition, Jews do not bring flowers to cemeteries, but instead place stones on the graves as markers. Because of the influence of this great, honorable man, many have chosen to write messages on paper, fold them up, and place them on the gravestone, just as Jews from around the world place notes in the Western Wall in Jerusalem.

After the collapse of Communism, many of those who had fled Czechoslovakia under the brutal regime chose to return to their homeland. The new government welcomed them back with open arms, and economic opportunity was now available to anyone willing to work hard. I wondered if I, too, could embrace living in Slovakia again, and tried to imagine what might entice me to stay. Perhaps falling in love with a Slovakian Jew who still lived there?

On one hand, I was aware that I could not escape my painful memories. On the other hand, I was swept up in the religious euphoria that was now being openly expressed in the country of my youth. Jews were suddenly free from fear of persecution. It struck me as strange that people no longer had to worship in secret.

According to the Torah, the essence of our faith is based on asking questions and seeking the answers. The search for those answers is a lifelong journey. This is not something you can buy in a store or have delivered to your doorstep, but a truth you have to discover for yourself. We are all responsible for finding our truth and for living our life in a manner that harms no one and helps those in need, just as I once was.

So who am I? In Slovakia I was called a Jewess, a euphemism for a dirty Jew. In America I was a young woman from Czechoslovakia. Now I am a Slovakian-American Jew.

I loved my house in Manhattan Beach, but I knew that the time had arrived for me to leave it behind. While I had once believed that I would either die in that house or have my cold hands pried off the doorknob at the age of 95, things had not panned out as I had expected.

I went down to the cellar and pulled out Harry's and my favorite Fleetwood Mac CD, "Rumours." As I danced in my faded wedding gown, I laughed and cried, soaking the fabric with my wet tears. I called the same realtor who had sold me the house 25 years earlier and told him that I'd decided it was time to sell. It turned out to be the green light he'd been waiting for, as he had a long list of interested parties.

I downsized to a two-bedroom apartment in Sheepshead Bay and offered up some of my furniture to friends and neighbors. Every day I would haul books, toys, and clothing to the picnic tables by the beach, knowing that someone would stake their claim and find in them the same enjoyment I once had. I watched little children shriek with glee as they discovered the goodies I no longer needed. As a woman and a typical Jewish mother, I felt even more joy than the children themselves.

I packed my extensive owl collection, as well as old photographs, Bohemian crystal glasses, vases and dishes, and my mother's most treasured coffee set into cardboard boxes. After that, as if written in a script, I packed my luggage once again.

I am a nomad, always on the road – a true Wandering Jew.

CHAPTER TWENTY-THREE

Festival of Light

Brooklyn, Winter, 2009

I have always loved candles. I keep them in nearly every drawer of my home so that my apartment smells sweet and fragrant at all times. The delicious scents carry me back in time, eliciting warm memories of days gone by. In addition to smelling divine, candles are also the symbol of holidays. As with other religions, there are so many holidays in the Jewish calendar year that it's not easy to remember them all, let alone observe them. But by lighting candles each and every Shabbat, as well as on Chanukah, we pay tribute to our ancestral traditions.

These candles are the manifestation of our adherence to Jewish law and custom. Throughout history they have served as symbols of the "Pintele Yid," the little spark in a Jew's soul that never abandons its connection to God and the Jewish people. Religion has always been of utmost importance in my life, and no matter where I found myself in the world, lighting candles represented that continuity of tradition. They also reminded me that even though I was far from home, the flames of family love still shone brightly.

One cold winter afternoon, I lit a candle in my living room and breathed in its sweet scent. As I observed the dancing flame, I silently prayed, meditated, and offered gratitude for everything in my life, both good and bad. I realized in that moment that I was no longer ruled by the sadness that had pervaded my life for so long. I could laugh more easily now.

Since that day, I have performed this ritual on a regular basis. It is my own method of prayer, and while I use my own original words, I still stay true to my Jewish roots.

There's an old joke, a definition of Jewish holidays that goes, "They wanted to kill us but they didn't succeed. Now let's eat." In fact, sometimes it seems like the only purpose of Jewish holidays is to eat. I have always enjoyed these festive gatherings of family and friends, and the food and the candles are an inseparable part of who I am and always will be.

Just like little girls the world over, I used to love to play dress up and sew outfits for my dolls. As I got older, I developed a taste for fashion. I couldn't get enough of shoes, dresses, bags, and fine fabrics. I never cared about the quantity, and it was only the quality that mattered. Routine life bored me; I always wanted to discover new things and accomplish new goals.

In essence, I am still that same little five-year-old girl from Porubka, walking barefoot in our courtyard, avoiding the chicken droppings and playing near the water well with my pail and shovel. I remember how I wanted to dig a hole deeper than the well, because America was at the other end. I didn't know much about this land of freedom, but I'd heard about it from my neighbors who had relatives there. I can clearly recall the time when some of those relatives visited Porubka and gave me my first piece of American chewing gum. How different they appeared from the people in my village. They had big smiles on their faces, and that's the moment my love affair with America began.

I still cherish the moments with family around the table, although they are not as frequent as they once were. I am now in my mid-fifties and am happy to say that I'm still surrounded by my sisters and their families, as well as longtime friends. I have traveled extensively, both inwards and outwards, and my sons are grown men on their own, both fine gentlemen. I have traveled a road filled with curves, traps, triumphs, and love. I also experienced the highest and lowest emotions of sorrow and joy, yet never once in my trials did I doubt the existence and presence of God in my life. I believe in him as strongly today as ever before.

I no longer cook to the extent that my mother used to, as I did when my family was younger. But I still enjoy preparing meals and sharing food with my family, friends, and neighbors. On Fridays I still look forward to the weekly Shabbat dinner. As I wait on line in the bakery for freshly baked challah, the aroma carries me back to my mother's kitchen.

The years, even the most challenging ones, seem to have flown by. I feel as if the boys were born just yesterday, with me changing diapers and Harry childproofing our home. Because they were born so close together, my sons kept us in a flurry of activity that I still remember as the happiest years of my life.

Now that my sons are men, I can only hope that my efforts to raise them alone have paid off. With some certainty, I think I can say that they did. From an early age, my boys learned and understood that although life isn't always fair, it is always good. *I* learned that I can't protect them from everything. I can only pray that any tragedy they face will make them stronger and better equipped to conquer life's inevitable challenges.

"Mom, you are so beautiful," David, my younger son, said one day out of the blue.

"Sweetheart, that is so kind of you. You used to tell me that when you were little and it always cheered me up." My mother's intuition told me that something more was going on here.

"Yes, but don't you think it's time to slow down a bit and enjoy all you've worked for your entire life? Have that piece of chocolate without guilt or feeling the need to run off to the gym. Just live like you tell me – 'nothing in excess.'" David smiled, as he gave me the ultimate compliment.

I was beautiful to him no matter what. Now I was sure I had done a good job. "Thanks, but you don't need to butter me up. Just tell me what you want," I said, laughing.

"Why is it that every time I compliment you, you think I want something?"

I knew he was preparing to ask me for something. It could be anything from borrowing my car to giving him extra money for an extended weekend in Miami with his friends. I knew him too well. I went from being the center of the universe for both my sons, to being their personal chef, taxi driver, ATM machine, and now their banker.

"Now that you have made me curious, give it to me straight. What is it this time? I know you better than you think," I said sweetly.

"I don't want anything," he said.

I knew not to push him any further. "Okay," I replied, and left it at that.

As he sat in the darkening apartment, typing something on his computer, I stood in the kitchen, secretly observing his profile. I noticed the gently pronounced cheek bone, the dark eyebrow, the droop of his eye, and the intensity of his mood. I wondered to myself who he looked like.

As he realized that I was looking at him, he became uncomfortable. No matter where I stood, he always seemed to hone in on me, and knew exactly what I was up to. He didn't like being stared at for any prolonged period of time. In order to break my gaze, he would make a funny remark, respond with a silly joke, or just smirk, staring back at me with a look that made my heart melt.

After a few minutes, the conversation picked up where it had left off.

"Mom, I hope this doesn't insult you, but you do realize you are one sexy mama?" he said.

"David!" I shrieked in shock.

"Yes?" he answered in his normal tone.

"You don't say these kinds of things to your own mother!"

"Come on, Mom, you're still young and attractive, and even if you don't think so, incredibly cool. But I feel like you're upset about something and I can't quite put my finger on it," my son said in a more mature manner than I had expected. "I just want you to assure me that everything is okay."

At that moment, Henry entered the apartment. "Hey bro, what up?" he said to his brother, in his best American slang.

"Nothing. You?"

Sensing he had interrupted a serious conversation, Henry asked, "What did I just walk into?"

"Nothing," I snapped back. "Everything is fine, I was just thinking."

"You always say that," David said.

"Exactly, Mom!" Henry added, not even knowing what the conversation was about.

"I have a vivid imagination that doesn't always serve my best interests. Let's leave it at that," I said, intending to end the conversation.

"Here we go again," Henry said, rolling his eyes and sighing.

"There is nothing I have to tell you. If there's something you want to tell me, or there's something that's troubling you, just spit it out," I said, trying to deflect attention away from me. "One day you will understand why I am the way I am, and it's not up for discussion right now. It also has nothing to do with either of you."

"Please stop talking in circles and just say what's on your mind. You're just like Bubbe Simone, always speaking in riddles," Henry said, continuing to push me. "Maybe Mom has something she would like to share with us," he added, as if he were peering right into my soul.

"Okay, I can't lie to either of you and I can't hold it in anymore. I got a parking ticket and I'm consumed with guilt. I miss the comfort of having someone ease my guilt. When Daddy was still alive, he would perform his magic, washing away all of my troubles just by telling me not to worry, that it was his ticket." I said.

"Mom, stop worrying. Now, it's our ticket!" my boys said in unison, and we all burst out laughing.

By that time, Henry was living by himself, and he looked forward to spending Shabbat dinners with us. Although born just one year and two weeks apart, Henry and David had such different personalities and temperaments. Of course, to me, they were both perfect. David had slightly more luxurious tastes, while Henry was more practical in his leanings. They both had fantastic, yet different, senses of humor, and were quick to tell or laugh at a joke.

Henry also had a sharp intellectual mind that astounded me. His vocabulary was vast and impeccable. Whenever I stared at him, all I could see from every angle was a young Harry, even down to his mannerisms. I loved both of my sons equally, and while they sometimes drove me up the wall, I still loved them unconditionally. I know that love is reciprocated.

I began to wonder what kinds of brides my sons would bring home. I even began to imagine their weddings. Who would be the first one to walk down the aisle? I wondered. Would their chosen ones be religious, modern, educated, attractive? Deep down, I began to obsess about it and soon realized that, oh my goodness, I had turned into my mother! The only difference was that I didn't have linens popping out of every drawer and closet for the dowry. I dreamed of the dresses I would wear at their weddings, but I never got further than choosing the colors.

Since an arranged marriage was out of the question, I hoped that they would find nice Jewish girls who they truly loved. In my own selfish way, I prayed that these future daughters of mine would come from intact families. After losing their own father at such tender ages, I didn't want my sons to be deprived of a solid father-in-law. At the same time, I left them to their own devices when it came to love and made up my mind to let them choose freely.

Like all single people, young single Jews are searching for their other half, their *bashert* – a kindred spirit who understands that a wedding is a day but a marriage is a lifetime. They are looking for someone who is willing to give one hundred percent of themselves, while expecting the same from a partner. This was my wish for my sons. I had no doubt that the day would come when I'd see them smiling under the *chuppa*.

These days, I pine to be a grandmother, especially after spending time with my sisters' grandchildren. But I know that life has so much more in store for me. For now, I'm just enjoying the ride. Some days I feel as if I'm being hurled back in time to when the boys were mere babies themselves. In those days, we would spend hours on the beach throwing crumbs at the seagulls, running from the incoming waves, burying each other in the sand, and building castles with our pails and shovels. I even have fond memories of trying to clean sand from every nook and cranny of their little suntanned bodies, including between their toes. Before they could enter the house, I'd hose them down in the backyard.

I recall the extravagant double birthday parties I would plan weeks in advance, down to the most minute detail. I would hire clowns, face painters, pony rides, magicians, blow-up slides and, of course I would bake plates of delicious goodies. Every child would leave with a smile, a full belly, and a hand- picked favor. As I entered the room with their cake, candles burning brightly, and I'd snap photographs of my boys as they blew them out, I would beam with pride. It was the same feeling I got on Chanukah, when I saw their tiny faces illuminated only by the light of the match I used to light the menorah.

When they were little, Harry and I used to give them gifts, one a night for eight nights, each gift carefully chosen and wrapped. Now that they are older, I mostly give them Chanukah *gelt*, or in simpler terms, money. But they are always grateful and we always enjoy lighting the candles together.

"It's the first night of Chanukah, time to light the menorah. The one on the far right," I said to Henry, who picked up the middle candle, called the *Shames*, and lit the first of the nine arms.

"Who wants to say the blessing?" I asked my sons.

"I do!" they both replied, sounding like eager little boys.

They wore the yarmulkes we'd had made for their bar mitzvahs in Israel so long ago. As they began to recite the prayer in Hebrew, we lit the candle together. There was something magical about this ritual. My sons smiled at me and I held both of their hands tightly, smiling back. It wasn't just a show I was putting on for them, but genuine love I was expressing. Unfortunately, they were at that age when they got easily embarrassed and they tried to wriggle free from my grasp.

Once upon a time there was a miracle. The Maccabees' oil was supposed to burn for one day but it burned for eight. We celebrate that miracle for eight days and eight nights, yet I couldn't get my boys to hold my hands for eight seconds! We celebrated anyways, and each night we added a new candle to the left side.

Henry became the official latke maker, having inherited his culinary skills from me. I would prepare the batter and he would fry them, flipping each one with care and attention. The whole kitchen would be covered by the grease that splattered everywhere, but it was worth it. His latkes always turned out delicious.

David was happy to be the official taster, offering his critique. He considered himself a latke connoisseur. These moments were so precious to me, and as I added marjoram to my batter, it reminded me of my mother's latkes, which I so loved and missed. Unlike most American-born Jews, who dipped their latkes in applesauce or sour cream, in our home we would eat them right from the draining towels we laid them in, after they'd been perfectly fried.

Latkes are considered unhealthy, not just because they're deep-fried in oil, but because of the fact that most of the oil remains inside of them. There is an old rumor passed through the generations that the Maccabees actually used a latke instead of olive oil that night. That's why it burned for eight days and nights, the same amount of time it took to get rid of their heartburn!

When I look at my sons today, I am the happiest mother on earth. I accomplished what I set out to accomplish all those years ago. I am a free woman in America, and a proud Jew. I overcame so much and am still standing strong, always looking for the next project to tackle. I still cry from time to time, but not as frequently. Tears contain the power of rebirth and are actually quite liberating. I believe that a person who doesn't know how to cry doesn't know how to enjoy life.

Together with my sons, I would like to commemorate my mother, Bubbe Simone. I still feel her presence every day and know that through-out my life, she blessed me and my decisions. I want to remember her preparing latkes in the kitchen, showing off her beautiful, golden challah, and proudly walking me down the aisle with my father at her side. I do not wish to remember her by that horrifying number A-9103 engraved on her forearm by the Nazis for all time.

I made it to America and proved that, yes, dreams really do come true. But I still have one more dream to fulfill. This time it's Harry's dream that the whole world will see what six million never could. I want the city of Kosice to honor Ludovit Feld's memory by exhibiting his works in a museum. That museum should carry the name of the little giant who was a savior to so many children in Auschwitz.

I also want a street to bear Feld's name or a monument erected in his honor, so that his memory will stand tall and live on forever. It is time for the city he lived in and loved so well to acknowledge his contributions to their cultural life. With his towering talent, this legendary dwarf bore witness to mankind's most horrific acts. He infused every painting and drawing, whether of his beloved city or of his unforgettable nightmares, with great emotion and detail. It is my greatest wish that Ludovit Feld, dear Uncle Lajos, gets the recognition he deserved in his lifetime. This is now my work-in-progress.

Epilogue

I AM BEYOND THRILLED TO share that in September 2015, together with the leaders of the Jewish community in Kosice, we established a cultural center of Ludovit Feld adjacent to the synagogue on Puskinova Street. The gallery centers on Feld's life and work as well as introduces to the public other Slovakian Jewish artists. Lectures on Jewish history and the Holocaust are also offered at the gallery.

In 2016, a life-size bronze sculpture of Feld, which I dedicated in memory of my dear husband, Ari Fishbaum, was installed on a pedestal in the courtyard next to his gallery. Finally, 25 years after his death, our Uncle Lajos can look directly into the eyes of his admirers.

I am looking forward to the upcoming dedication of a park in the beautiful old city of Košice which will bear Ludovit Feld's name.

Famous photo of Ludovit Feld (front, left) leaving Auschwitz Concentration Camp, 1945. Feld is 40 years old at the time of this photo, seen next to a six-year-old twin boy who was among the many victims of the infamous Dr. Josef Mengele's sadistic experiments.
(*Auschwitz-Birkenau Memorial and Museum*)

A snapshot from my recent visit to Slovakia next to the life-size sculpture
of Ludovit Feld, our "Uncle Lajos," by artist Professor Juraj Bartusz on
Puskinova Street in Košice, Slovakia.
Dedicated in memory of my beloved husband Ari Fishbaum.
(Photo: Eva Timurova 2017)